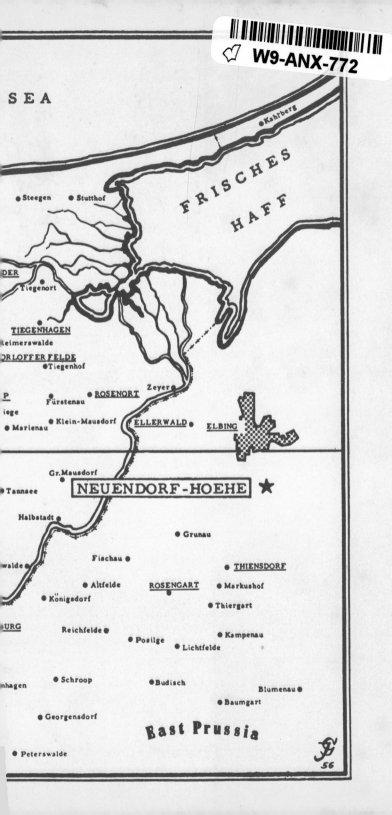

Nightmare in Red

Horst Gerlach

Creation House, Inc.
Carol Stream, Illinois

FIRST EDITION

Library of Congress Cattalog Card Number: 77-131447

Printed in the United States of America

CONTENTS

Chapter

INTRODUCTION

Some men are called of God to live through traumatic experiences and, by an experience of faith, interpret these for the benefit of their fellows. Dr. Horst Gerlach is one of these men. I first met him soon after his release from the prison camp in Russia when he came to Eastern Mennonite College as a student. Serving as campus pastor at the time, I had the privilege of counseling him in his commitment to Christ and instructing him for baptism in the Christian church.

Through the years, it has been an inspiration to see the depth of his conviction and to be enriched by the perspective which he brings to events which are facing us in these times. The background of his experience subsequently interpreted through his commitment to Jesus Christ points the way for others to be discerning, to forgive their enemies, and to commit themselves to God's work of reconciliation in the world.

Dr. Gerlach's Prussian background has conditioned him for a disciplined life; his early involvement with Hitler's youth group and subsequent disillusionment have transformed his thought; and his commitment to Christ has given him a spirit of compassion for society. All of this has enhanced his discernment in evaluating movements today. While it will be difficult for some readers to understand all that he shares, it is not difficult to sense his faith and directives for Christian living today.

This book is a contribution from one who is committed to radical discipleship in following Jesus Christ, but who is neither radical nor reactionary as he interprets the Christian's place in history. The proof that he has overcome the trauma of the experience in his late teens is in the effective service which now characterizes his life as a scholar, educator, and churchman. His book should serve as a stimulus to our faith as we face the stresses of a tangled world.

MYRON S. AUGSBURGER, PRESIDENT
EASTERN MENNONITE COLLEGE
HARRISONBURG, VIRGINIA

Memory's eye view of the farm in East Prussia where the author lived as a boy. In right foreground is the farm house; next around the circle is the granery; then the stable and the straw shed. In the center is the wagon shed, and the chicken and hog house is in the foreground.

Drawing: Jan Gleysteen

1

BOXED IN

The nightmare I am having is real; it is complete in all its dimensions, even to the stereo sound track. I hear in the background the chorale of death, a monotonous accompaniment of hopeless sounds.

Click—click—click; click—click—click. Am I dreaming or is this reality? A cold draft blows over me. Once again I am back in a bleak boxcar hurtling deep inside a province of Russia.

I pull up the thin cover I was fortunate enough to have brought along, and I try to sleep. But rest evades me. All my limbs, joints and muscles ache from the constant lying, sitting and standing of the trip. No other position is possible; the space is too small for my body.

Not by turning my body nor by any other effort can I ease myself into the much-needed healing sleep which might allow me to forget everything for awhile. Sleep when it does come is not oblivion; it is a time of unwelcome dreams. My mind has not been able to accustom itself to the chaos that now surrounds me. Only rarely does a dream occur that concerns itself with the present. When that comes it projects the horror of the past weeks; what took place then is indelibly etched upon my subconscious.

Lying in the half dusk, I see passing before me all the happenings of the war's end and of my country's collapse. It is as clear to me as if everything had taken place just yesterday. Even today, many years later, these impressions stand out vividly. The stark tragedy of my experiences plagues me yet.

EARLY IMPRESSIONS

Since my birth on February 5, 1929, my world had revolved around farmhouse and school. I lived with my family and our helpers on a farm near the village of Neuendorf-Hoehe, where the inhabitants were either farmers or worked for farmers. My father was himself a fairly successful farmer owning a two-hundred-acre farm.

During my growing-up years the politics of our country were a foreshadowing of what was to come. The German people had already been blessed by a man who was, by his own self-acknowledgment, our "messiah." He had risen over the years from the office of corporal in World War I to the position of Chancellor in the Third Reich.

It was natural, then, that I became a member of the Hitler Youth like all the rest of the German children. It bothered us little that we were being prepared for later military service. As young boys we played warlike games outdoors without weapons, and aggression was taught as part of our schooling.

As I grew older the significance of the work I was conscripted to do did not impress me. I and the other youths shoveled dirt obediently, feeling a little like children still playing soldiers. Only the discomforts of the life we were forced to accept really bothered us. Living in tents for months, with a brook for our washbasin and the earth as our table, we constantly complained about the inconvenience.

8

We learned military discipline early. "Attention, eyes ahead, report, eyes right." These, the commands of the Hitler Youth leader to whom we answered, play back loudly in my memory. They carried across the drill ground to where we stood, uncomfortable in the hot August sun. But we held ourselves erect, facing the future. The year was 1944.

Our laborious work of digging trenches was assigned while we were students ranging from fourteen to seventeen years of age. It was a lesson in endurance to make men of us.

Victory was confidently assumed by us. Belief in the invincibility of the German race was an inbred part of our character. The fact that the Russians had penetrated into the border at the eastern part of our homeland did not alarm us. Neither did the first frightful reports which filtered back to us.

PREPARING DEFENSES

That year marked the beginning of what was going to snowball into a major offensive. Oblivious, we worked on through the weeks as the summer changed into fall. By October we were beginning to suffer from the cold, and the ease of working in the ground was affected. The process of excavating the trenches was becoming harder; as we dug, masses of sand continually slid down. Finally we employed a system of revetment and began lining the fortifications with young trees. This was a successful method, but only until every pine tree in the surrounding area was used up.

The racial mixture of our construction gang was colorful, to say the least. A Ukranian company built the bunkers. A combination of Latvian SS (*Schutz-Staffel* or "protection force"), Hungarian OT and a former antiaircraft construction company of captured Badoligio Italians, all helped in the building of the *Ostwall* or fortification against the Russians. Surprisingly enough, we boys were the only Germans represented in the projects.

I believe today that the experience of these early days enabled me to survive later inhumanities and hardships. Normal human feelings were squeezed out and I early learned to be concerned only about myself.

Other credit must be given. In the gruesome and dangerous events of my later life it would almost seem as though I had been singled out by some destiny to live—to live in, through and out of the unbearable.

I had been given the upbringing of a stalwart Nazi. Along with the rest of the East Prussian people, I had become used to a strict administration, but it had usually been one with some understanding. Transition into the Nazi regime came gradually. The Nazi administration was not totally liked by the people for many reasons. It became the source of unending jokes and rumors, the only course of active resistance possible.

Hardly anybody knew then that Hitler's headquarters was not far from Rastenburg in East Prussia. After the events of July 4, 1944, his residence there was not so secret, for news of the assasination plot attempted that day was widely publicized.

The hearts of the women and children and the older people were filled with deep concern because of the harsh treatment given to the Germans by the invading Russians. But we boasted about the "miracle weapons" which had been employed by the Germans. Our work of constructing fortifications seemed useless to us. We believed our country was safe, and in our minds we were convinced that the Russians would never come close to our hometown in western East Prussia.

SITUATION WORSENS

After the abortive attempt to take Hitler's life, the "Führer" let it be known that a "miracle of divine providence" had spared him. In an attempt to squelch the troublemaker, Colonel Count Stauffenberg had set off a bomb in Hitler's office.

It did seem as though circumstances spared Hitler's life. On the day of the assassination attempt, his bunker was being repaired and he was using makeshift quarters. The bomb went off with much less effect in the lightly built barracks used for his staff meetings than it would have had in a concrete pillbox. Several officers were killed, but Hitler was only slightly wounded. The explosion merely lifted the oak table on which he was leaning at the time.

Hitler's officials were disliked by the people and were of little service to them. Nazi governor Erich Kock, one of the most corrupt, was supposed to have been shot in 1935 for lining his pockets with money collected for the poor. He had no training for his position besides his natural greediness. A former railroad employee, he compensated for his lack of experience by the use of rhetoric and a pretentious manner. As a practice he removed good administrators and promoted inadequate ones. Even criminals were advanced to the highest offices; the only prerequisite was that they be subservient to him. This was a virtual betrayal of the people's trust. Obviously the officials trusted by the administrative mayor were not able to tackle the problems created by emergency situations.

This failure soon became apparent from the turn of events. In August, 1944, the state capital, Koenigsberg, was attacked by two hundred British bombers, followed by another attack of six hundred bombers. Most of the inner city was destroyed, with 35,000 civilians killed and 150,000 left homeless. Several sections of eastern Germany were overrun by Russian tanks. The newspaper reports carried alarming stories of the massacre at Nemmersdorf and the accompanying rape and bloodshed.

In reflection, I realize anew how great were the difficulties which began to confront us. But at the time I was pre-

11

occupied with my occupation; I was still under conscription and hard at work building fortifications.

Greater difficulties came to me and my fellow workers with the cold weather of the fall. About this time we were briefed about the situation. Without a doubt the Russian offensive was looming over us. It was no longer unavoidable; we would have to cope with the impending invasion threat.

The Russians outnumbered the German troops ten to one in Eastern Prussia. Our invincibility could no longer be assumed, and we were taken to a classroom for instructions. Our teacher was a former major who had just been released from the army because of his wounds. Standing before the class while resting his right elbow on the windowsill, he presented the situation in a matter-of-fact way. As he began to speak, silence descended over the listening group. I felt my pulse accelerate with suspense.

"The Russians are beginning an offensive," he stated. "They have an overwhelming superiority in men and material." He hesitated before continuing, although no one had interrupted him.

"The Russians," he went on, "are constantly gaining ground. Our soldiers are fighting the hardest contest of this war. Let us hope that all will turn out well."

Looking out the window and not at us, the old soldier seemed to be talking quietly to himself.

"The situation is very serious and I'm afraid—that—all—is—lost."

His words caused even the most optimistic among us to have grave thoughts. My heart sank as though in premonition of what was to come.

2

PREMONITIONS

The major's words kept ringing in my ears after we were dismissed from building the fortifications and allowed to return home. Events there were appearing to bear out his statements. Since the beginning of autumn, refugees had been moving westward. These same people had earlier fled to the east to escape the bombing raids of the Americans and English. Now they were returning to western Germany because the Russians were advancing from the other direction. The first refugees from the East Prussian border— mainly women and little children—accompanied them. The stream of refugees grew larger each day.

As the news from the front lines became increasingly ominous, our family and some of our workers began to pack up. Unexpectedly a great snowfall descended. Because of the previously mild weather, our horses had not yet been roughshod. The milk truck which had daily hauled the milk from our farm and the neighboring farms of our village to the dairy in the city suddenly ceased coming. Supposing that the snow had caused this, my brother and I took the milk to the dairy on a sled. There we saw troops with cartridge belts, camouflage coats, and hand grenades. A panther tank stood before the city. Seeing such well-equipped soldiers, I was overtaken by a definite feeling of calmness; the soldiers were well prepared and victory seemed assured.

My brother and I had hardly returned home when my father gave us another job to do. We were to ask the smith whether he could roughshoe our horses. I went to his shop and found that the blacksmith was sick.

"I can't shoe them. I'm sick!" was his reply when I inquired.

"But the apprentice? Where is the apprentice?" I asked.

"He did not come to work today," said the master, shaking his head.

I had to return home, unsuccessful in my errand. My father was becoming increasingly troubled. He thought it would be a good idea for one of us to ride over to the home of the smith's apprentice who lived with his parents about two miles from our village. I resolved to take the apprentice to the smithy.

RESIDENTS FLEE

Along the lane and then out on the highway, I rode past a seemingly endless train of refugees. At the home of the apprentice I jumped off, tied the horse, and knocked at the door. I knocked softly, but there was no answer; then harder, and again there was no answer. Finally I knocked as loud as I could. Nothing stirred. Then I noticed that the door was somewhat ajar. *Strange,* I thought, pushing it open. I slowly walked inside and looked around; nobody was at home.

Going outside again, I knocked at several neighboring houses. The result was always the same—nobody was at home. In one backyard I noticed a pool of blood. I stopped short and wondered. And then everything became clear: the inhabitants of these houses had butchered their swine in a hurry and then had fled. The nearby manor house was also empty. As I walked slowly and thoughtfully through the open rooms, I heard nothing but my own steps. An uncanny feeling overcame me and I hurried outside.

As I left I could hear the cows lowing in the stable of the estate, obviously aroused by my horse's hoofbeats. *The cows are still there?* I asked myself. *Of course,* I reasoned, *the fugitives must have left their cattle behind.* The complaining, bawling sounds continued as the animals appealed for food. *Should I feed them?* I thought. *No, I'd better go home first.*

I decided to ride diagonally across the fields to get there quicker. Afterward I looked around anxiously to see whether anyone had noticed my detour. As I saw the smooth snow-covered fields lying before me, I realized there was no longer anyone around to challenge my crossing through the fields, which was usually forbidden.

At home everybody was hastily packing. Our house was a scene of great disorder. Carpets had been torn up and laid on wagons in preparation for the flight. Silverware, dishes, pictures and food were stowed away. At my father's command, everybody was packing parcels to carry along for our daily needs.

Father was very troubled when he heard my report. Since our horses could not be roughshod, our flight was questionable, for the roads were very icy and unusually slippery.

The telephone was in constant use. Either we were calling neighbors or they were calling us for advice or something else. The military news report informed us that the Russian troops were already at Osterrode which was only sixty kilometers distant. But since this announcement was apparently a day old already, we assumed the Russians were closer still. Or had they been driven back in the meantime? Did we still have a chance? These were questions we wanted answered —our lives depended on them.

EXPLOSIONS AND FIRE

Toward evening we heard explosions in the distance. We thought perhaps they had been set off by our retreating

15

troops. Refugees came driving to our farm with their wagons and requested a night's lodging. Explosions were constantly being heard. Southward, the evening sky began to grow red, undoubtedly reflecting the glare of fire. Were the Russians already in Prussian Holland, the area that was only twelve miles from us? We still could not hear infantry fire or grenades, and the telephone was still ringing and being used.

We went to bed without undressing. It was difficult to sleep because torturing thoughts and inner unrest kept our tense nerves from relaxing. The next morning the sun rose on the horizon, spreading a reddish glow over the snow-covered landscape. A thick hoarfrost hung on the branches and telephone wires.

Farm duties were tended to and the cows were cared for as usual. After the milking was finished, the milk for the dairy was then poured into cans. The effort was fruitless because the milk truck failed to appear. In perplexity my father decided to call the dairy. He raised the telephone receiver but the operator did not answer and the phone seemed dead. So Father sent me to the public long-distance telephone which was about a kilometer away. I buckled on my skis and left in a hurry. As I sped along, the snow creaked and a flock of crows passed by cawing. When I arrived at the site of the public phone, I found that the telephone there was not in operation either. No one at the post office, where the phone was, knew what else to do.

Meanwhile, at regular intervals explosions occurred, apparently not too far away. I was inquisitive and wanted to investigate the matter thoroughly. Slowly I pushed myself forward on the skis over the gently ascending roadway until I reached the position where only a small ridge separated me from the next village. No sooner had I arrived where I could see unhindered than I was frightened by a sudden burst of fire and the subsequent thunder of a cannon. Like a phantom I could recognize the contour of a tank with its cannon muzzle pointed at the nearby city.

That must be the Russians! I thought. *The cannon thunder at night must have come from rear-guard fighting.* I realized that the low-trajectory tank shells had not produced the usual whining sound of cannonballs. On the German side hardly any infantry or artillery had been employed, for most of the soldiers had retreated down side roads. Consequently the nocturnal cannonading had come only from the Russian advance-guard tanks. I found out later on my journeys in captivity that this assumption of mine was justified. Empty tank-cartridge cases were lying around everywhere.

TRAPPED

A new outburst of fire from a Russian tank interrupted my reflections. The tank stood right at the intersection of our side road and the main road; thus we were completely cut off from our escape route. Flight was no longer possible. It was too late. There was nothing left to do but to turn around and go home.

On the way back I again went past the post office where I had tried to use the public phone. Everything was in tumult there. The reason for the chaos was the presence of four German soldiers who had waded through the deep snow from the highway. Fatigued to the point of exhaustion, and driven by strong fear lest they should be captured by the Russians, they said the Russians had broken through to the nearby city of Elbing and that its encirclement was imminent. Hearing this, I flew down the hill toward home as fast as I could.

On the way I met a number of trek wagons. The anguished travelers had no map, were not acquainted with the area, and had been wandering about in circles. Despair swept their faces as I explained where the Russians had already invaded. They had come hundreds of miles, successfully avoiding both the Russians and any battles, but now fate with one merciless blow had frustrated all their efforts.

Back home in my village I extinguished the last sparks of hope when I shared the news of our impending encirclement by the Russians. In this sea of disappointments the only plank to which we still clung was the hope of a German counterthrust. The Russians who were near us thus far consisted only of spearhead tank divisions sent in advance of the main army which was attacking from the southeast. Neither infantry nor artillery had accompanied the tanks, and without these a complete penetration of the area was impossible.

I could not stay at home very long. Young as I was, I felt compelled to seek new adventures. This time I chose to set out in the opposite direction. Outside our village was a single farm whose owner had leased out a smaller farm on the highway. Near the main farm I met the owner's son. We exchanged greetings and recent experiences, and he told me that the Russians had made the tenants of the smaller farm give them their watches. The thought that this might be awaiting us caused me to shudder, dreading that the Russians would likely serve us with worse cruelties.

I quickly left his farm and turned back, taking a shortcut through the fields. Here I discovered footsteps in the snow. Supposing they had been made by fleeing German soldiers, I followed them until I came upon an old military overcoat. I picked it up and examined it. In one pocket I found a big onion and, beside it, a Russian Soviet star! Apparently a Wlassow soldier had lost this coat from his pack or had thrown it away as too heavy for the flight.* Several days earlier I had met many bands of retreating Wlassow soldiers. The owner of this coat must have pocketed the Soviet star

---

* These soldiers were Russian volunteers who served in the German army under the command of the former Russian General Wlassow. Wlassow was later on captured by the Red Army and executed for high treason.

in case he had an opportunity to transfer back into the Russian camp again.

I smiled. But instantly I remembered the badge that I wore on my cap as a member of the Hitler Youth. I took it off and put it in my pocket. I put the newly found Soviet star there too. I thought wryly that these symbols of two diametrically opposed world views would have to endure each other in my pocket.

Dejection

For the noon meal I was back with the family again, but none of us had any appetite. We had the dejected feeling that we were eating our *Henkersmahlzeit*—the last meal of the hangman's victim. The German propaganda in press and radio, and even eyewitnesses, had prepared us abundantly for our "liberation," or rather, for the people who announced themselves as our "liberators." As it turned out, these self-appointed Russian liberators far surpassed in actual practice what the German propaganda had led us to expect of their behavior.

Since our cowhand with four other villagers had been called to the *Volkssturm** and had gone to Elbing, we had to go to the cow stable after dinner in order to care for the cattle. While doing this work I felt somewhat easier. Everything was rather quiet, and I was glad that through this diversion I was at least delivered to some extent of the anxiety which had recently oppressed me.

But this feeling of relief was not to last long. Villagers came to our farm to report that the Russians had taken the watches from all the inhabitants in the post office vicinity. In addition the Russians had indicated that by evening our

---

* Semimilitary organization, created at the end of the war. This unit was composed of men who were of pre- and post-military age and was an emergency measure of the German government.

19

village would be occupied and that all who possessed weapons would be shot.

My father threw his army pistol into the snow behind the house. I hid our hunting weapons in the loft of the pig stable. Then Father, who knew from both the First and Second World Wars how the Russians loved both watches and boots, made my brothers and me put on our boots. I guess he supposed that they would be safe because the soldiers would not take the boots off our feet.

Later that afternoon we suddenly heard overhead the subdued regular humming of airplane motors. *Probably German fighter planes!* I thought. We ran out of the house and looked up. Nine racy Messerschmitts had come to provide an offensive. With incisive attacks they bombarded the Russian spearheads with machine-gun fire and bombs. After awhile the planes resumed formation and disappeared northward.

3

INVADERS

"The Russians are coming!" I don't know who first cried out those words in wild fear. I do know that for us East-Germans they marked the beginning of a seemingly endless hard time of suffering. These words for many were also the final message before a submachine gun blast from the "liberators" stretched them out in their last sleep.

"The Russians are coming!" The forewarning announcement was true. Slowly and always on the alert, the Russian, for there was only one, came with gun held in readiness and with a heavy tread along the lane and up to our farmstead. Fifteen pairs of eyes—of my parents, my brothers, our employees and myself—followed his every movement through curtains and door cracks. I involuntarily thought of my new boots and whether or not I should have camouflaged them. I quickly wrapped old dirty rags around the boots and rubbed the ramps in the dirt behind the house.

Meanwhile the Russian came nearer, paused, scanned the place, and came a few steps closer. At first he was

21

headed in the direction of our house; then he hesitated and walked across the yard to the wagon shed. There he sat down on a wagon tongue.

My mother told us boys to go to work in the stable, because the soldier would then think we were farmhands. Consequently I left the house, kept close to the granary, and hardly turned my head toward the soldier.

But he had seen me. He called out something that was unintelligible to me and made signs with his hand that he wanted me to come to him. Somewhat nonplussed, I pointed questioningly at myself. He nodded, and since there was nobody besides me in sight, there was nothing left for me to do but to obey his invitation.

Alternate hot and cold surges raced along my backbone as I approached him. I realized that I would not be the first German shot down by a Russian in cold blood for no reason whatsoever. But nothing like that happened.

I eyed the Russian distrustfully. A fur cap sat back on his head. He wore a three-quarter-length fur overcoat that was held together by a broad leather belt, in the middle of which was a Soviet star. His quilted pants were stuck into dirty felt boots. His face was typically Mongolian. Under his felt cap hung pitch-black hair.

While the Russian kept his left hand in his pocket, his right hand pointed a German .08 army pistol at me. For a few moments we stood in silence. Then he started talking with words which again I could not understand and which he underscored with wild gesticulations of his pistol. It seemed to me that some of his words sounded somewhat like a few words in Polish that I had learned from our Polish workers. After a time it became clear to me that the Russian wanted cigarettes.

I had both hands in my pockets. In one pocket I happened to have a package of *Attikas,* a German brand of cigarettes, which I had recently found. I shook my head and asked, *"Chlebba?"* which translated means bread.

The Russian pointed with one hand to his neck, as if to say, "Full up to here!"

Inwardly I had to laugh at my diversionary tactic. Still I felt somewhat odd, for I realized he intended to search me.

Meanwhile several other people from the farm had come up to where we were standing. Among them was a Ukrainian refugee who began to converse with the Russian. I seized the opportunity to leave, without any further incident.

A LONG NIGHT

The night came on. Everything was trembling from the roaring of cannons or from frequent explosions. The other boys and I didn't want to sleep alone anymore in our own room so we crept into our parents' bedroom. It was not like an ordinary time to retire and nobody undressed. By the dim light of a kerosene lamp we huddled together, two of us for a while on a chaise lounge, and all of us tried to sleep. Father blew out the light. But even in the darkness we didn't rest for a long time.

In the adjoining room refugees were lying down — old men and younger women with small children who had requested shelter. The children were screaming and everyone was talking. We were all too worked up to calm down very early.

Outside, the cannonading gradually lessened and at last ceased entirely. It was now so quiet that one could almost have heard snowflakes fall. Was it a calm before the storm, a calm that might be more disquieting than the storm itself? An uncanny foreboding came with the stillness, an apprehension born of uncertainty as to how this all would turn out.

Suddenly an attack broke loose! Rifles, automatic pistols, and machine guns rattled. The sound of weapons was everywhere and it was constantly coming closer! Again a brief silence. Again a new outbreak! Now sounded a confusion of voices. Were they German? Were they Russian? Then

23

the house door creaked. Somebody was walking clumsily around in the kitchen, then in the dining room. It was a shuffling sound, as if someone were prowling around over the floor in house slippers. Our suspense mounted higher and higher. My entire body was trembling. It seemed as if everything was falling to pieces in my brain. Atrocity stories which I had heard about the Russians went tumbling through my mind.

CONFRONTED

A beam of light seeped through the keyhole of the bedroom door. Something was thrown against the door and it was flung open. The glare of a flashlight shone harshly on our faces. Under its cone of light the barrel of an automatic pistol gleamed. The shaft of light played inquiringly about on the walls and furniture of the room then came to rest again our faces.

In the dim reflected light I discerned two fur caps with Soviet stars. It was the Russians!

My father understood some of the Russian language as a result of experiences in the last war. He was able to answer in the negative to the question the Russians asked as to whether there were any German soldiers in the house. Even though my father denied their presence, the room was immediately searched. Bedcovers and pillows were lifted, the space under the beds was searched with the flashlight. One Russian looked intently at my brother who is two years older than I. I was also inspected carefully. He could not believe that we were not soldiers.

My brother, born in 1927, had already reached the stature and also the age of a soldier. However, in 1944 at the close of his work service, he had suffered a compound fracture of his shinbone in an accident. The injury was so severe that he was medically exempted from further drafting. Fortunately he found his most recently removed plaster cast which he could present as evidence to the Russians who were still searching the rest of the house.

I repeatedly had to explain to the Russians on my fingers that I was only fifteen years old. I later learned the necessary Russian words.

The only German word that the two Russians knew was *Uhr,* meaning a watch. They pronounced the word gutturally so that it sounded more like "Urr." My father's gold pocket watch, which lay on his bedside table, became their first booty. Otherwise everything passed off fairly well this time. After they had looked around for some booty among the refugees in the next room, the two visitors disappeared just as suddenly as they had arrived.

Our first closer contact with the Russians had ended, and I felt somewhat relieved. Nothing had happened to us and, except for my father's watch, we had lost nothing; the uncomfortable feeling of living in a no-man's-land or in the battle area was past.

For awhile peace reigned in the house. Only outside in the yard did I hear the shuffling of felt boots now and then. But, after an hour or two, things broke loose anew. One after another, there appeared groups of two or three men, generally drunk or under the influence of alcohol. There were men with friendly faces, others with countenances distorted by hatred, including Asiatics and Russians, all apparently twenty to twenty-four years of age. Some resembled bears. All wanted watches. Only thousands of watches would have satisfied them all. It was as if the Russians had expected the Germans to provide the whole Red Army with watches. When they asked for watches and we answered that we did not have any, they threatened us with their burp guns. They behaved quite savagely. Then they found some liquor in the living room, and after the alcohol had done its work, they rummaged through our property and turned everything upside down. In one of the closets they found part of an old uniform that my father had worn in World War I. Since these things looked so colorful, they thought they had caught a general. They hauled my father out of bed, dragged him into the living room, and demanded that he account for it. Only with much labor was Father able to convince them that these insignias belonged to a long-past era.

Continual Threats

During all that night we were threatened by Russians. Some locked us up. Others came and were angry that the doors were locked. Everything was moved around, lifted up and looked through: chests, suitcases, boxes. The contents were scattered on the floor and some things were taken.

Two Russians had searched the cellar early in the night, then locked the door, and thrown the keys away. Later when another group came and found the cellar door locked, they supposed some unknown danger lurked behind it. Accordingly, they fetched my father; in order to avoid execution he broke the cellar door open with an ax and they sent a machine-gun blast down the stairs to prepare for the search below. My father, who had been dragged out of bed again, was made to walk before them in case someone hidden in the cellar would shoot at them.

In the meantime there were motor cars crossing the yard. We heard commands and calls. Then everything became still with a dead calm—no sound far and wide. I held my breath and listened anxiously, trying to hear out into the night. There was nothing. Suddenly, with an immense flashing, a murderous roaring began. It was as if the whole world was coming to an end. We had the bedroom perfectly darkened. Only through the heart-shaped cutout in the shutters could we see the reflections of gunfire. We crawled close together and watched. How long the inferno actually lasted, I do not recall, but it seemed to me like an eternity. The flashing slowly ended with a whistling sound and a rushing-away noise which lost itself in the distance. Then in the direction of Elbing we heard hollow explosions.

My thoughts went to the city and the soldiers of the German occupation toward whom the assault was directed. My father, experienced in things of war, had no idea what kind of weapon was involved in this nocturnal concert.

As the night progressed, our "guests" became more intoxicated by the hour. They fidgeted around with pistols and guns, talking to us sometimes for several minutes in the Russian language, apparently oblivious that it was unintelligible to us. Father had instructed all of us to answer any question with the phrase "Nie pononeisch," which means "I don't understand."

Another group had dragged a record player into the house and were playing it in the adjoining room with screaming and a lot of noise. It seemed that for hours we had to listen to the jazz music accompanied by the singing of the drunken Russians. Women and girls were brought in to satisfy their terrible desires. Everything was upside down, but this time the wrong side was up.

Toward four o'clock in the morning the liquor had overcome them. The noises gradually ceased. Our so-called liberators had dropped into a deathlike sleep, each one just where he had been carousing. The house stunk as if the plague had been there. The odor of gasoline, dirt and vodka penetrated the rooms. It was disgusting.

During the first night that the Russians were there the so-called "Stalin Organ" pulled up behind our straw shed. It could not be aimed precisely, but this unpredictability made the soldiers jittery.

Drawing: Jan Gleysteen

4

UNDER OCCUPATION

We dozed restlessly until about six o'clock in the morning. Then Father told me to get up and go to find the Polish laborer who was to work in the cowshed. I didn't want to go very much, for the fear of the night had not yet left me. But I finally got up and put my overcoat on. It was pitch-dark. Would the Russians do something to me? Carefully I stepped through the rooms. In the dining room the three record-playing soldiers were sleeping, heads on the table, in one hand a machine gun, in the other the vodka bottle. I stopped a moment at the door and listened before I dared to go further.

In the outbuilding adjoining the kitchen in the back part of the house stood a guard. He seemed to be guarding the cars and trucks which stood outside in the snowstorm, about twenty yards away. He did not want to let me pass, evidently because he thought I might be a German soldier who had put on civilian clothes. Only after I explained to him at length what I was going to do, did he let me pass. I don't know whether he really understood or not. Shivering, I walked through the deep snow. My attention was attracted by our skis which lay askew in the snow and had been hacked in pieces. I passed the plundered wagons of the refugees and the careless disarray of their property which the Red soldiers had scattered all over the yard during the night. Beds, boxes, feathers, paper, silverware — all were lying in the snow. The wind was whirling snowflakes into the damaged wagons.

In the apartment of the Polish family, the same picture met me. A drunken Red soldier was sitting on a bench, leaning on his gun, sleeping. The Polish people, who also had been hardly able to sleep, seemed to have had the same experience as we during the night: wine, women and brutality.

The cowhand told me that he would soon come to the barn; I then went to the cowshed and began feeding the cattle. By and by, all the farm's inhabitants assembled in the stable, for most of them had heard that it was safest to work — the Russians seemed to respect workers. And this surmise later proved to be true. As soon as we began to milk the cows, a stream of Russians appeared to get milk for themselves. The visitors kept increasing until there was almost no milk left for us or the calves. The experience taught us to use crafty means in the following days in order to save enough for our own household. This was necessary since there were a few small children among the refugees. When I walked over from the barn to the straw shed I saw the war artillery which had caused the murderous firing during the night. Mounted on the back of trucks were what looked like eight railroad tracks, each about five yards long. From the top and the bottom of the back end hung two four-foot-long rockets. It suddenly dawned on me that this must be the "Stalin organ," the famous invention of which our soldiers had talked during their furloughs at home. The Stalin organ was actually a rocket gun which could fire sixteen rockets over a very short period of time.

Thoughtfully I walked across the yard toward the wagon shed where some of our flight wagons had been stored for our escape to the west. Here I saw the same picture of destruction. I gathered up some documents which were lying around in the snow and in the melted water and carried them to the house. They were some of our saving accounts from the bank and other valuable papers.

BRUTALITIES

As time progressed, we received more horrible news about our surrounding neighbors. One farmer, who had been the fire chief of our village, had shot his own eighty-eight-year-old father to death before committing suicide. He did not want to become a prisoner of the Russians. His wife and daughter had been bound to a bed and used by the Russians fifteen times. Another farmer's wife whom the Russians had been trying to rape, had jumped into a well where her doleful cries were soon quenched by the icy water. Later on the Soviet soldiers pulled her body out of the well and threw it on the manure pile. Her fourteen-year-old niece was stripped and raped by the Russians in front of her mother. In order to escape further torture, some refugee families had all entered a room and turned the gas on. Some more compassionate Russians happened to come upon them, opened the windows just in time, and they regained consciousness.

A twenty-five-year-old man who was dumb, had been shot to death. The Russians supposed he was a soldier whose silence was an act to escape being taken prisoner.

Our neighbor's wife was shot through both hands. Her daughter-in-law escaped through a window with her eight-day-old baby and hid in a strawpile to escape rape. Another farmer's wife died in despair when her oldest son was killed in action and her husband and her only other son were deported to Russia.

31

Another farmer's widow was killed by a bullet fired from a strafing fighter bomber. She was hit in the abdomen and endured unspeakable pains till she passed into eternity. She left four children. One was taken into French captivity; another had to flee without shoes when the Russians tried to catch him. But they caught him later anyway. The other two children, still rather small, were taken care of by other women who had survived. The family of our teacher was completely wiped out. One son was shot down over England, another fell on the eastern front, and the teacher and his wife were taken away, never to be heard of again. The fate of our grocer's family was similar. The parents were deported, one son was killed in action, and only two sons survived. In all the farmers' families in our village, all the husbands were deported or killed. Only one survived the captivity in Russia.

Often the soldiers separated mothers from their children to take them to Russian camps. Many died on the way to the camps, while others died at home, having been infected with venereal disease which rapidly spread after the arrival of our liberators. One woman who had worked for us lost three daughters. One died at home; two were shipped to a concentration camp in the Ural Mountains. Two of my uncles were deported and died. One of my aunts jumped with her baby into a lake to escape constant raping.

HORROR CONTINUES

The following nights and days were a repetition of the first night. There was constant racket. Russian soldiers came and went, looking through everything and using the available women and girls. Between these periods we often watched the firing of the Stalin organ whose strategy we understood now. Just before they fired the guns, the soldiers usually started to scream; we figured out later that this meant that everybody had to assume safety precautions for no one was allowed to be close to the guns while they were fired. The rockets were fired by remote control. They took off with a terrible noise and left a trail of fire. Thus one rocket after the other was shot. Several minutes after they were in the air, one could still see them on their deadly mission to the city. I believed (and soldiers later verified it as fact) that it was very hard to hit a particular target with this kind of gun. Rockets from this piece of artillery could cover a very wide territory; thus the soldiers who were firing it became jittery because of its unpredictability.

Later on the situation quieted down a little. It seemed as if the Russians had done the most necessary jobs. Only a few guerillas came to our farm for girls, watches and jewelry. The partisans, or we might better call them parasites, were soldiers who had left the army and tried to enjoy the war. Most of them were fellows without any conscience who shot whenever it appeared necessary to them; however, as soon as a Russian officer appeared, they left by bike more quickly than they had come, heading toward another territory to continue their destruction. Our house was gutted in a matter of days. It smelled like a cesspool. My mother and some of her hired girls cleaned it from top to bottom to make it livable again.

In those days the Russians seemed to enjoy riding bicycles. It seemed as though they had found a new national sport. Most of them had never sat on a bike before. To some it made little difference whether there was air in the tires or not; the main thing was that the wheels turned. The Mongolian soldiers had the most fun with them. They would sit for hours on a bike and ride back and forth on the road.

Our column got larger on the way to Prussian Holland. They picked up everybody who could walk. Sometimes they put the children of two mothers together and took one mother along to Russia. Burned tanks lined the road.

Drawing: Jan Gleysteen

5

GERMAN STRATEGY

The Fourth Army under General Hoszbach, who was one of the most able generals the army had, tried right from the beginning to avoid being encircled by the Russians. In order to permit escaping to the west, Colonel Schoepffner was given the order to defend the city of Elbing. With the few troops he had, he did an excellent job. We had dug trenches around the city, but in order to man them, three divisions would have been needed and Colonel Schoepffner did not have even one. So all he could do was to post his defenders at the city's outskirts. In a later report of the happenings on January 23, he wrote: "I received a phone-call, 'Enemy tanks have just passed the army barracks and are proceeding toward the center of the city.'"

He quickly mobilized a few squads to destroy the tanks. His biggest worry was that the masses of refugees who were waiting in front of the railway station to be evacuated to the west might be fired upon by the Russian tanks. He heard detonations originating from firing tanks and exploding bazooka rockets. And soon he was notified over the telephone

35

that four tanks had been knocked out. The three others had left the city through the northern gate.

The commander of the city defenses asked himself the question, "How could it be possible that seven Russian tanks could pass the defense lines without being noticed?" His probings revealed the following: The Russians had apparently moved along with the refugee vehicles on the road which led from Prussian Holland to Elbing. In the dusk and the general mix-up, the people had taken them for German tanks, since the crews wore German uniforms apparently stripped from German soldiers. As soon as they had passed the main defense lines, they thought they could take the city by surprise. They were apparently aided by a man who knew his way around.*

But although the destruction of these tanks boosted the soldiers' morale, thousands of refugees were overtaken by panic and tried to leave the city where temperatures sank as low as 22° below zero. Finally the Nazi party decided to order the people to leave without providing any leadership themselves. But it was too late for an orderly flight. This proved that the party was unable to tackle the problem, and it clearly exposed their lies about an eventual German victory.

The Russians succeeded on the 24th in bringing more tanks to the outskirts of the city. German defenders in the city had to rely on soldiers who had been on leave and could not make it back to their units. The local gun factory produced several artillery pieces for a few units, thus helping to buttress the local defenses. From the Baltic Sea the heavy cruisers *Lützow* and *Prinz Eugen* engaged their heavy guns on Russian troop concentrations, the fire being directed by an artillery officer in the city. By and by, when the weather began clearing up, the Russians used armored fighter bombers to attack the city. Houses were burning, and whole

---

* Kurt Dieckert and Horst Grossman, *Der Kampf um Ostpreussen* (München: Grafe & Unzer, 1965), pp. 105f.

streets were reduced to rubble. The civilians who could not make up their minds to leave the city when it was still possible, sat in their cellars awaiting their fate.

The Russians used bullhorns manned by German-speaking soldiers, asking the defenders to quit fighting and come over to them for a good meal and honorable captivity. Finally, they sent to Colonel Schoepffner several German peasants who made fantastic promises to him in case he would surrender the city. He refused the offer but issued a paper to the brave men, saying that they had discharged their duties. They had to return because the Russians had threatened to shoot their wives if they did not come back.

From our home we saw German dive bombers bombing Russian troop concentrations. When the Russians saw them attacking, they fled into our basement. The Soviet soldiers, who always appeared to be brave when dealing with civilians, were suddenly cowards when confronted with a real fight, for some of the dive bombers were just a hundred yards away. I was actually able to see the pilots in the cockpits.

THE COUNTERATTACK

General Hoszbach had earlier conceived a plan of forming a circle, with the refugees in the middle, and then breaking through to the west and uniting with the German forces west of the Vistula River. According to this plan, his divisions would have to move on icy roads, hindered by snow, snowdrifts, and miles of refugee columns to the west. He managed to do so in four days. The Russians were attacking from the east, pressing the troops hard. Hoszbach ordered his troops to dispense with everything not absolutely necessary for the retreat, with the exception of ammunition and food. He chose a moonlit night for the breakthrough to the west since the Russians could not use their superiority of tanks, infantry and air power during the night. Furthermore, the Russians, who often did attack during the night, were usually poor fighters when they were attacked in a nocturnal assault. When the German troops attacked Guttstadt they found many Russian soldiers in bed with women they had just raped.

During the night of the attack, the snow-covered scenery was lit up by the moon. Without firing a shot the Germans started out at 7 P.M., after having marched 150 to 180 miles without rest. But thus they succeeded in completely surprising the enemy.

Russian troops and artillery were destroyed or captured. The 170th Division alone captured ninety-six Russian artillery pieces. The soldiers also saw the atrocities the Russians had committed in the occupied villages. In one of them they had run a youth over by tank just because he wore the emblem of the Hitler Youth. They found the body of a young woman on the manure pile with a knife in the chest. In one village they had shackled several men, poured gasoline over them and burned them. In a third village was the body of a dead girl who had taken poison after having been raped fourteen times.[*]

It must have been around February 1. As we were working in the cow barn in the morning, we suddenly heard rifle fire at the entrance of our village. Soldiers in white camouflage dresses were rushing over the snow-covered fields.

While we heard the noises of armored vehicles from the main road connecting Elbing and Prussian Holland, a smaller detachment had apparently been ordered to probe the eastern flank and make sure that the exposed left flank of the counterattack would experience no surprises.

My first reaction was to start toward them to see for myself what was going on. My father must have noticed my intention.

"What are you trying to do?" he asked.

"Oh, I just want to walk over to the soldiers and see what is going on."

_____

[*] Ibid., pp. 115 ff.

"I think you're not quite normal," he retorted. "Do you want to get hit? Go to the haymow and throw some hay down for the cows."

Up I went. But before I threw the hay down, I peered through an opening in the wall.

The shooting had slackened momentarily. The soldiers had surrounded one of the first houses. Then they opened up fire again. I didn't want to miss that. At last, German soldiers again! I think I never threw hay down as quickly.

As soon as my job was done, I looked around for Father. Not seeing him, I took off in the direction of the soldiers. Crossing fences and hedges, I finally arrived almost breathlessly at their position. When I came closer, I saw that the patrol was composed of ten to twelve men, most of whom were infantry, and some soldiers whose blue uniforms were covered by white camouflage suits and snow caps. They were led by a lieutenant.

"Are there any Russian soldiers around here?" asked the lieutenant.

"They were here yesterday," I answered, "but I did not see any today—at least not a unit."

"What do you mean by no unit?"

"Well, you know yourself that there are usually a large number of men who leave their outfits. They conduct their own war, with plundering, raping and so forth."

"We have met only little resistance so far, but there are certainly some hanging around," he continued while looking toward the next farm. A machine gun took up position on the road and a few soldiers were sent to investigate the buildings.

After awhile, rifle fire, intermingled with a submachine-gun blast, resumed. A few soldiers soon came down the lane escorting a Russian soldier with his arms raised.

"What was he doing there?" the lieutenant asked the soldiers.

"He has been molesting the women," replied the nearest.

"What shall we do with him?" asked the other soldier.

"We don't have enough men to escort him back, so go ahead and kill him," commanded the lieutenant. The soldier who walked behind the prisoner ordered the Russian to march on. The captive Russian seemed to suspect something, for he looked anxiously around and started to weep.

Suddenly the escorting soldier raised his burp gun, and a hail of bullets hit the Russian in the back. I turned away. When I looked again I saw the Russian sprawled in the snow, reddening it with the blood dripping out of his mouth and nose.

The counterattack went on. The next farm was searched. There was the bursting of hand grenades and the breaking of window glass. The machine gun was on the road and ordered to give fire protection for the advancing soldiers.

Soon I noticed that a Russian soldier, probably made curious by the noise, came riding toward us along the street on a two-year-old horse. The German soldiers were camouflaged pretty well. Only if one were standing close by could he see the German army caps under the white of the camouflage jacket. And, often the Russians used these same jackets after they had stripped them off dead German soldiers, so it was rather hard to distinguish between friend or enemy from a long distance. "Let him get closer," ordered the lieutenant. The Russian came riding toward us confidently; one hand was on his hip, and he was looking as proud as a general—until he was about fifteen yards away. Then he must have noticed something, for with a wild cry he jumped off the horse and ran away. But the machine-gun blasts were quicker than he. With a terrible cry, which I shall never forget, he sank down into the snow and was dead.

After this came a dispatch rider. The spearhead which had been advancing along this side road was called to retreat to the main road to join the central body of the army. This was quite a shock to us. Many of the villagers were standing around the band of German soldiers. Most of us had thought this would bring us relief—that they would enable us to retreat to West Germany now. We were especially fearful because we knew the Russians would retaliate for their lost companions if they returned to our village. What were we supposed to do?

"Take some food along with you and go to the fortress of Elbing till everything is cleared up from the enemy," the lieutenant told us. And then the men retreated.

Meanwhile a number of villagers, women and children, had gathered. Now since the soldiers were gone, these people became even more fearful than before.

"When the Russians come back and see these dead ones, they will think we did it," said an elderly lady.

"And they won't believe that we didn't do it," added another.

"Well, come on, let's bury them in the snow," I suggested.

"That would be a good idea," said the elderly lady.

I jumped over into the ditch and tried to clear away enough snow so that there would be enough room for the dead soldier. Then we lifted him over and covered him with snow. Having finished this, we went over to the other one and proceeded in the same manner. Then I went home.

"Where have you been?" asked my father.

"Well, I—I—I—wanted to see the fighting."

"And get killed," scolded my mother.

"But I was real careful." I tried to belittle my disobedience. "When they started to shoot, I hid behind a big tree."

"Next time, you stay here, or else!" ordered Father angrily. "War is no child's play."

He was right on this score. I had seen that much.

Then he wanted to know what the lieutenant had said.

My father was not too much in favor of the advice of the lieutenant, since we had daily witnessed that the city was constantly attacked by fighter bombers. Also he remarked

41

that if the counterattack succeeded, the area would be mopped up soon anyway. In any case, going toward the city was unjustified.

FAMILY DECISION

Part of the villagers, however, started out the same morning toward the city. My father still rejected the plan. Finally, at about four o'clock in the afternoon, he decided to follow our neighbors to the city. We loaded up sleds with food and blankets and started to drive toward the city. On our way there, the thunder of the guns became louder and louder. Apparently the German counterattack had met hard resistance. We found out later that the German army which had been encircled in East Prussia tried to escape toward the west. The general in charge was General Hoszbach, the former adjutant of Hitler. A very gifted general, he tried to have two army divisions at the front, one in the north and one in the south, and to have two in the back. The East Prussian refugees, who numbered several million at that time, would be in the middle. It was his plan to bring all the refugees safe toward the west.

However, the Nazi *Gauleiter* of East Prussia, Erich Koch, informed Hitler concerning the intent of his army commander Hoszbach. Hitler ordered two divisions of this army for the defense of Koenigsberg, the capital of East Prussia. At that time many Germans still believed our country could win the war. The propaganda ministry under Dr. Joseph Goebbels had told them so often about the coming wonder weapons, and had urged the people to endure so that they would be available in order to smash the enemy. Thus it was thought that as much of the German territory as possible should be held till this day would come. Anybody who gave up was called a coward, and many were executed even in those last days when there was no longer any hope. Hoszbach's plan to bring as many refugees as possible safe to the west ran completely counter to this Nazi plan.

Therefore, Hitler ordered Hoszbach to the west, where

42

he was flown out of the completely encircled East Prussia, and General Müller was appointed as his successor. Since two divisions were moved to the defense of Koenigsberg, the force of the counterattack was broken and the Russians repulsed them. The Germans now say that the operation ran out into the sand. It was found out later that the *Gauleiter* himself had been fleeing from the Russians, and was riding on a German navy icebreaker in the Baltic Sea on his way to the west. Governor Koch sent Hitler this telegram: "General Hoszbach and the Fourth Army on flight to the Reich. They cowardly tried to reach the West. I defend East Prussia with the Volkssturm!"

The Russians finally had enough troops concentrated to halt the German counterthrust. The divisions of the Fourth Army being on the constant move for days without sleep, and taking heavy losses in severe battles, were finally repulsed.

CATASTROPHE AT SEA

Several hundred thousand refugees had fled to Koenigsberg and Danzig in order to reach a ship of the German merchant marine or navy, to be evacuated to Denmark or western Germany. However, those who could not make it anymore were for the most part taken prisoner by the Russians or murdered. In Roessel County, at least 524 persons were murdered. In Loetzen County the Russians murdered fifty-two persons, among them eighteen French prisoners of war. In Mohrungen County the Russians deported 50 percent of the civilian population.*

Ports on the coast north of Elbing were crowded with refugees. To eliminate the congestion, the German merchant navy used its biggest ships to transport them. These vessels had been converted into hospital ships for the most part. Refugees and wounded soldiers were moved on them to the west. Such ships as the *Wilhelm Gustloff* (25,480 tons),

---

* Ibid., p. 128.

Robert Ley (27,000 tons), *Cap Arkona* (27,000 tons) and *General von Steuben* could take as many as 12,000 refugees. The disheartened refugees who boarded them expected to be relieved, finally, from their sufferings. But the large ships with their big superstructures were an easily recognizable aim for Russian submarines and aircraft. One of my aunts was on a ship that was strafed several times by Russian fighter bombers. The *Wilhelm Gustloff* left Gotenhafen on January 30, 1945, with about 5,000 refugees and soldiers. She was only accompanied by a small torpedo boat. Most of the people on board felt that they were safe at last when suddenly at 9 P.M. they were shaken by a tremendous explosion which occurred near the coast of Pommerania. The lights went out and a few seconds later the boat was hit a second and then a third time. Doleful cries could be heard from the lower decks, and sticky clouds of smoke billowed through the ship. Three Russian torpedoes had ripped the hull open. The ship started to capsize.

People panicked and began running. Those who fell were trampled underfoot. Terrible scenes could be observed as many fought desperately for the lifeboats and rafts. Others slid down the icy hull of the capsizing liner only to reach the below-zero water. Emergency signals lit up the sky, and a few boats rushed to their aid. The fog horn sounded three times. A little later the ship capsized and sank to the bottom of the Baltic Sea. There was a gush of water, then silence. Only 904 persons could be saved. Some who were found sitting up straight in boats were already dead when rescue parties tried to hoist them aboard the ships that had rushed to the scene. The rescuers discovered that the survivors had reached the lifeboats only after having been in the icy water. After they had crawled with their soaked clothes into the lifeboats they froze to death within a matter of minutes.

The *General von Steuben* was hit by several torpedoes fired by a Russian submarine, even though the vessel was painted white and clearly marked as a hospital ship. She sank within twenty minutes, carrying with her 2,700 people to the bottom of the ocean. Only 300 refugees and crew members could be saved. It was impossible to rescue the seriously wounded because of the speed with which the ship sank.

The *Goya,* however, met the biggest catastrophe. This ship left the encircled city of Hela on April 16, carrying 385 slightly wounded soldiers, 1,500 soldiers and 3,500 refugees. At midnight the ship was hit by two torpedoes fired from a Russian submarine. The ship broke apart and sank within a matter of minutes. Escorting ships could save only 165 people and this time 5,220 perished.*

SENSELESS ORDER

Any further attack to the west was stopped by Hitler three miles short of Prussian Holland. General Müller was now in command. According to General Groszmann, he was later handed over to the British, who in turn handed him over to the Greeks, who executed him for misdeeds committed during the occupation of Crete. Müller had had only twenty-four understrength divisions for the defense of East Prussia. They had to face one hundred Russian divisions and a number of well-equipped Russian armored divisions of the second and third White Russian front. Because of this senseless order, hundreds of thousands or even millions of soldiers and civilians had to suffer a terrible death or to be kept in prison camps for years and years.

Some refugees had tried to retreat over a lake and thus get to the west. The ice broke and many of them went to their death in the cold waters. Besides that hazard on the ice, they stood out as better targets for Russian machine guns

---

* Ibid., pp. 129 ff.

and fighter bombers. After the war we learned that the general himself went to Denmark; later, by dressing in civilian clothes, he hid himself among the people of north-west Germany. Several years later, however, he was detected by a few people who recognized his familiar face and he was deported to Poland to be tried there. He had committed several other crimes while being in charge of the eastern part of the Polish and Russian occupation during World War II.

Halfway to the city we met the mayor of our village; he was on the way back home again. He told us that just as he was entering the city, a fighter-bomber attack began. The occupants had to jump off the sleds and hide behind house ruins in order not to be shot to death. After this had happened several times, the mayor decided to return home. Father turned the horses around and we also went home again. The Russian fighter bombers were flying overhead about twenty yards above us. They were so low that we could see the pilots looking out at us.

The next night we went to the cellar to sleep, for the thundering of the guns kept on with the same force. We were all afraid as we listened into the night. I don't know how late it was when I heard some steps above us in the house. I wondered: *Is the visitor a friend or an enemy?* The steps retreated. Peace and quiet returned. But it wasn't long before the noise started again.

The night visitors seemed to be more careful this time. After they had searched the rooms in the house, they came down the steps toward the cellar. Flashlights searched the area. Two hard-bitten faces of Mongolians were looking with mistrustful eyes toward all of us on the straw bedding. Their faces brightened when they noticed there were girls among us, and they ordered the girls to accompany them. The cries of the girls made me tremble as time after time that night they were forced to go upstairs with the men. The so-called "liberators" were back again.

46

6

DEATH OF A CITY

After the Russians had repulsed the German counter-attack, they tried to conquer the city of Elbing with all their available power. Every evening we saw the flames lighting up the clouds with the red glow which proclaimed the death agony of the city. Flames were eating up street after street, church after church, building after building. Fighter bombers attacked day and night, and the resistance did not seem to be very strong. The only other heavy artillery stationed in the city were six batteries of immovable heavy-aircraft batteries. Some of my fellow students were stationed at those batteries. They tried to defend the city as long as possible.

The Germans inside the so-called "fortress" of Elbing, although very short on heavy weapons, tried to do their best. In their operations they used several captured Russian tanks. The German swastika flag was placed on them as long as they moved in the city. It was removed as soon as they went into operation outside of the city. Thus they fooled the Russians and caused a lot of confusion among the enemy. The Russians made a mass attack around the airport against the German machine guns but were repulsed with heavy losses. Refugees from the city told us that the Russian soldiers had been mowed down by the hundreds.

Heavy cruisers from the Baltic Sea tried to support the city garrison by shelling troop concentrations around the city. But one day a flight of nine German *Stukas* or dive bombers circled over us and then started to dive and bomb troop and artillery concentrations. None of these maneuvers by either side helped to bring the war to a victorious conclusion.

Behind our farm several batteries of heavy and light artillery were readied and then were used to shoot into the dying city day and night. I remember one morning when a light-artillery battery arrived on our farm and started to set up its cannons right in our apple orchard. Since these cannons, the so-called *ratch-bums*, had a very fast, low-flying shell, the soldiers cut down all the trees in our orchard which were in the way. They could have easily installed their guns some other place but it never bothered their conscience to waste anything. The united effort of fighter bombers and artillery converted Elbing from a flourishing eastern city into a heap of ashes. The Catholic church in the middle of the city burned down completely, and many other famous landmarks disappeared with it.

Meanwhile the Russians advanced further and further into Elbing. The number of its defenders became smaller and smaller. The civilians could not retreat with the soldiers and, thus, most of them fell into Russian hands. Some of the inhabitants from our village who had been walking toward the city during the counterattack, now began returning to our village. Soon they circulated the news throughout the village of the Russian cruelties they had witnessed. Our neighbor's wife had been carrying an iron cross of her son's in her pocketbook. When the Russians found this

German decoration, they ordered her out of the building and shot her to death on the spot. Another neighbor lady had been shot to death while looking out the window.

Ammunition in the city became scarce. The Russians conquered city block after city block, committing unspeakable atrocities whenever they happened to run into civilians huddled together in the basements, civilians who had missed a chance of leaving for the inner city with the retreating soldiers.

Finally Himmler acted. He was the notorious chief of the SS who had been running German police and concentration camps and to whom Hitler had given charge of the army group in East Prussia toward the end of the war. Himmler issued an order for the defenders of the Elbing fortress to leave the city. On February 10 our troops of 3,200 men attacked the Russian lines, breaking through the encircling ring of the enemy and taking with them 850 wounded and a number of women and children. Thirty burned-out enemy tanks and thousands of dead Russian soldiers were left behind. Elbing, founded in 1237 by Teutonic knights, and a city with a population of 100,000, had been reduced to rubble within three weeks. Burning houses and smoldering churches continually lighted the sky. Sometimes the soldiers set fire to houses during the night in order to see better in case the Russians planned a surprise attack.

The Russians took their revenge among the civilians. A few SS guards were caught in the county prison and massacred there by their merciless conquerors. If a regular soldier did not expect much mercy from the Russians, an SS soldier could not hope for anything.

What motivated the garrison of Elbing to defend itself so long is perhaps hard to explain. If the war could not be won anyway, why did they not surrender? Every German soldier realized if he were captured by the Russians, he most likely would be killed right away or would have to suffer a terrible life in one of their notoriously bad prison camps. Even though there was no hope for winning the war, the soldiers defended themselves as long as they had weapons and ammunition. Their hatred for the Russians had risen to the highest pitch toward the end of the war. Pardon and mercy had become unknown words on both sides.

The number of people who lost their lives in 1945 is hard to assess. Groszmann estimates that of 2.6 million people who lived in Eastern Prussia, a total of 511,000, including soldiers who were born in this province, lost their lives in 1945. This was one-fifth of the population. There had been civilian losses in 1914-15 when the Russian troops occupied two-thirds of East Prussia. Their destruction and atrocities in the various areas depended largely on the individual troops and their commanders. But the senseless destruction of human life in 1945 was ordered by the Russian government.

FATHER'S DISPLACEMENT

In the meantime the Russian police (GPU) started to work among us. In the beginning we couldn't distinguish them from the fighting army. Because all Russians wore similar-looking topcoats it was even hard to differentiate the officer from the soldier. Only later we found out that the GPU wore blue stripes instead of red stripes like the soldiers.

By that time my father had become quite thin. The tremendous stress that had come upon his soul had carved deep lines in his face. For nine years he had lived the life of a soldier, fighting on all the fronts of both world wars, faithful to what he considered his duty.

He had hoped that now since his sons were growing up, they soon would be able to stand at his side and help him on the farm. Because he was growing old the Russians dealt with him as if he was worthless. I can still remember the particular day when three Russian officers came into our house and asked all kinds of strange questions. When they left, other soldiers came. One day while my father was

50

standing in the kitchen, he was surrounded by a whole gang of drunken soldiers. One of them decided to shoot at him for the fun of it. But while he was aiming and was almost ready to pull the trigger, another soldier pushed his hand so that the bullet went into the ceiling. How it happened that the other one jumped in just at that moment, we did not know. It never occurred to me that the providence of God might be operating in our behalf at this point. When we heard about the incident, I headed toward the barn as fast as possible. Even while I was walking across the yard, a tricky, husky fellow was aiming in my direction with a gun, but another soldier kept him from shooting.

The same afternoon several officers appeared, coming into the cow barn and watching us at work. Then they asked Father to go with them. I stayed in the barn until an unexplainably restless feeling surged up within me. I couldn't remain there longer. As if I had foreknowledge of the approaching events, I put the hayfork aside and walked over to the farmhouse. I found Mother weeping in the living room. With a look of unutterable sorrow she motioned toward the window. I looked out and saw Father walking away down the lane, escorted by two Soviet officers. This was the last time that I ever saw my father.

It was such a nice evening in February when he left that he failed to fortify himself with either blankets or food. Mother told me later that the Russians had found out after a short interrogation that Father had been an army captain and that he was a farmer. Identification as a farmer carried special meaning to the Communistic Russians. For them, all landowners were capitalists, and to the Communists this is a thorn in the eye. But the two officers who took my father away had promised Mother that he would be able to return soon.

My eyes burned. I would have liked to weep like a little child because of Father's departure, but I could not. I tried to comfort my mother somehow but I did not believe in his safety myself. Even today I can see my father as he walked away from us—without having said good-bye to his children—straight and determined, even in this moment an example of courage to us. It was February 4, 1945. I don't think that date will ever vanish from my recollections.

MY FIRST DISPLACEMENT

The next day, February 5, was my birthday; I became sixteen years of age. However, when the Russians later asked me for my age, I still said fifteen. This fabrication was an effort to escape capture. I hoped they wouldn't take young people with them.

Our food supplies dwindled. The Russians had acted like wild animals when they came to the various farms, wasting food senselessly. Flour, butchered pork, canned goods and many other things were lying around in the yard and the hogs were rooting in them. Since the sun was warm in those days, the food had started to spoil, and soon there was a rotten odor all over the farm.

Our main diet was vegetables which we got out of fruit jars. The Russians had been mostly interested in meat and had left most of our canned vegetables untouched. Whenever any of the Russians decided to eat some vegetables, they made one of us boys or my mother taste them first to see if they were poisoned.

More and more Russian foot soldiers came to our village. This traffic slowed down soon and after awhile the supply units moved through. There was quite a difference between the front-line soldiers and the soldiers of the second line. The former were usually young, strong men and fanatical Communists; among those of the second line were more elderly men with more common sense who had better understanding of our misery. Some could speak German. Although even these soldiers of the second line stole and butchered chickens, hogs and sheep and other animals

52

which they could find, they acted more humane toward us than the others had. The roughest gangs were those between the ages eighteen to twenty; they were always trigger-happy and molested the girls frequently.

But in general we were not as afraid of even the front soldiers as we were of those who were taking people away as prisoners. They were human headhunters, the most dangerous people among the Russian soldiers. Those who captured prisoners, interrogated them, and then sent them to camps in Russia were known as the NKWD. We realized that it was not wise to keep on living in our farmhouse. The Russians were molesting us there quite frequently because they did not like the capitalist class which we represented to them. After Father's displacement, we retreated into emergency quarters in our granary. From there we observed how all the cattle, which had formerly been a source of great pride to Father, were taken away. Over years of breeding he had developed a very high-quality breed. When the Russian soldiers came into the barn, untied the cattle and drove them away, we were helpless.

The Polish laborers who lived on our farm got passports from the Russian commander and moved away. We had to watch silently when they took our best horses and our own flight wagon and left. One of the horses came back a few days later. Probably the Russians had taken the horse away from the Poles, had used it a few days, and after that had turned it loose again. By some means this horse had found his way back home.

In the meantime we caught horses which were running around in the field and put them in the barn with the few which remained. The Russians came back often and got those they liked best, even some of the two-year-old *Trakehner* which we had never used yet and who were still unbroken.

HEADHUNTERS RETURN

Then one day the headhunters appeared again. We had

heard rumors that they would catch people only to deport them to Russia. We saw them come to the house where our workers lived. My anxious mother heard them and gave orders: "Quick, hide yourselves!"

"Why should we hide?" was my reply. "I'm only sixteen!"

"You are so tall and besides you remember that they once mistook you for a soldier," she insisted. I remembered the occasion and was wondering what to do when suddenly my brother took me by the arm and said, "Come, let's go hide in the haymow."

We climbed the ladder to the loft. I looked for a hole under a crossbeam and, seeing one, crawled in and pulled a bundle of hay over my head. I breathed heavily. The smell of the hay almost suffocated me.

Remember when Russian soldiers with their king-size bayonets pierced the hay and straw for hidden treasures? I thought.

The idea of being stabbed did not leave me. My brother seemed to have the same thought. After about fifteen minutes we both crawled out of our hiding places.

Just as we peered through the cracks down to the deserted farmyard, we heard the crunching noise of felt boots on the snow. Several Soviet soldiers in earthen-brown uniforms slowly walked over to the farmhouse and entered. In a moment the door of the house opened. Out dashed an elderly refugee lady. She ran straight toward the barn.

"Come down quickly!" she cried from a distance.

"Why don't you keep your mouth shut?" retorted my brother. "They'll catch on that we're here."

"They already knew that," she replied breathlessly.

"Well, did *you* tell them where we were?" I snapped.

"No, they found it out from the neighboring house by just casually asking whether there were any men around here. They sent me here to fetch you. If you don't come down from the haymow right away, they will get twenty soldiers and set fire to the barn."

I looked at my brother and his desperate face told me

that there was nothing we could do. Slowly we walked over to the house. Everybody was upset. The commanding officer sat in my father's chair. When he saw us, he snapped: "It's good you came, otherwise it would have been too bad for all of you."

The officer gave an order to the interpreter who relayed it to us: "I give the both of you fifteen minutes to pack your things!"

"But why pack our things?" I asked, acting a bit dumb.

The interpreter put on an ironic smile and said: "Well, you will be feeding cattle for six days and then you will come home again!"

"But I am only fifteen," I replied, while my tears almost choked my throat.

"And I was run over by a motorbike," replied my brother. And having said this, he rolled up his trousers to show them his cast. The officer looked at it suspiciously and asked my brother to come nearer.

After examining the cast, he told him: "*Carashow,* you may stay here. But you—" and he nodded in my direction, "will have to go."

He did not need to nod. I turned around and went to the kitchen, where Mother was busy preparing dinner.

I did not need to tell her much of what had happened. The Russians had already selected two girls who had worked for us in the home to go along and had ordered dinner.

We sat down and ate, although the food did not taste very good. Then they took two of our best horses and hitched them to one of our buggies. I said good-bye to my mother. She had tears in her eyes. I too could hardly refrain from weeping. I tried to be a man and comfort her: "Well, they said we will be back within six days!"

"Do you believe that?" she said with a despairing look. Because I could not answer, I turned away. I heard an elderly lady, who had worked for us for over fifty years, saying: "Oh, may the Lord bless you, Horst!" The old lady was a very pious woman. She had often baby-sat for us when we

55

were small. Even during the Nazi period she used to attend
a Sunday Bible study conducted by an itinerant minister.
Her words rang for a long time in my ears.

APPREHENSION

I turned away and followed the officers. I was filled by
many feelings I didn't want to show. The evidences of
brutality on the roads as we passed along horrified me. One
German soldier lay crushed by the tracks of a tank, his exposed entrails mingled with bits of shredded uniform.

Finally we arrived at a stop for the night—an old school.
About fifty of us were locked in there. In the entrance hall
in front of the classroom sat a group of Russian deserters
recaptured by the soldiers. They were busy taking the boots
off a German civilian. One Russian tried on the shoes and
found that they did not fit. So he tore the leather lining out
and forced his feet inside. Nobody interfered with his
actions. The guards permitted stealing from the German
prisoners by their countrymen.

Through the window I could see that there were dancing
flames shining on the horizon. Residents of the local area
who were imprisoned in the school with us told me that the
Russians had gone from farm to farm and house to house
setting the buildings on fire, and that more than half the
village had been turned into ashes already.

Then the interpreter announced that he was ready to be-
gin the interrogation. Each of us had to individually step before him. I reported that I was fifteen years of age and that
my occupation was that of a cowhand. I realized it was a
crime just to be a farmer's son.

"Have you been in the Hitler Youth?" he asked.

I shook my head negatively. "I have been a member of
the German Young Folk."

He shook his head as if in disbelief and put it down on
paper. He did not know what to do with that answer. The

56

"German Young Folk" was actually the younger section of the Hitler Youth, but I did not want to tell him that and he had not asked.

The next day the partisans who had been continually stripping the German civilians of their belongings were called out and moved to a different place. With the other Germans I remained three days there in Wolfsdorf-Höhe. Meanwhile our number had increased. When we were lined up we numbered a column of about two hundred persons, women and men. Our ages ranged from thirteen up to seventy-eight years. Our names were taken down and then we were counted. After that procedure we started marching in the direction of Prussian Holland. The guards were a few Poles who spoke broken German. We marched quite a distance that day and arrived at a village about two miles from the city; there we spent the night. It was terribly cold. We men had to move to the attic and try to sleep there. I tossed back and forth and could not fall asleep very early even though I was overtired. When I finally did drop off, I slept so soundly that someone had to pull on my feet to waken me.

The next morning we had to march to Prussian Holland, with the Russians following in their buggy close behind. When we arrived at Prussian Holland we had to wait with other columns of civilians on a nearby meadow. The guards had difficulty keeping the single columns from mingling with one another. Across from us stood a great three-story house in the style popular at the turn of the century. Hundreds of civilians looked out of the large windows. I saw familiar faces. The young girl who had been in charge of our village post office was among them. I nodded to her. The distance was too great to speak. Moreover, any communication was strictly forbidden.

RELEASE

We waited for hours without anything happening. I felt as if I were freezing, and stamped my feet on the ground to

57

try to get warm. Suddenly I heard from somewhere the number fifteen. *Does that have something to do with age?* I wondered.

I made elbowroom for myself and went up to the discussion group. Actually it was only the situation of a fifteen-year-old girl being questioned whether she wanted to go back home again. She was still too young. But the girl refused to go; she preferred to remain with her friends. She said that sooner or later the Russians would probably ask her to leave again.

I went up to the translator. "I am also only fifteen years old," I said. He looked at me and was astonished at my large size. He seemed to doubt me but then he looked and searched around in my papers and found that my claim was justified. He told me to go to the side of the group. I could not go home right away. I must first have documents. Hours later, when all the civilians had been directed into the house, then it was my turn to go with the buggy back to Schlobitten.

I received a handwritten passport. Gratefully I shouldered my knapsack and marched quickly away. I did not want to go along the streets for I feared that I would be seized again. Detachments went continually up and down the streets to catch people and make them prisoners.

I went along the railroad track, and passed several railroad buildings where the Russians were busily sending German grain to the east. Seeing me, one officer called to me. I went over to him and silently showed him my papers. He fetched some guards and insisted I go with them. I was dismayed but didn't protest. They put me into a nearby post office where I was shown into a small room with another prisoner. Another guard took up a place before the door to prevent our escape.

This guard looked like a good-natured man, chubby and harmless as a teddy bear. He kept coming in and offering us cigarettes. My cellmate, whose experience was similar to mine, chewed the cigarettes while I puffed at them in order not to offend or anger the guard. Around noon the guard brought us a pan with ham and a little bread.

Shortly after the midday meal, I looked through the window and discovered that the guard was no longer at his place. I pressed on the lock of the cell door. The door was not locked. The opportunity seemed one of those that comes once in a lifetime. If I believed in God's providence at this time I would have given Him the credit.

Cautiously I crept outside. There was nothing to be seen. Looking far and wide revealed no guard. I bent slowly forward and pretended to be exercising. Noticing that absolutely no one was observing me, I ran impulsively to the command post where I met the Russian officer who had issued me my passport. I spoke to him. He understood no German and I knew only a few words of Russian. He only shook his head in wonderment and shrugged his shoulders. But suddenly he recognized me and understood my gestures, and went with me to the post office. There he told the men who had taken away my papers that all should be given back to me. Then he nodded to me. I was again free. Heaven must have opened up that prison. The coincidence was unbelievable.

This time I hurried on my way as fast as I could. I wanted to get quickly away from that inhospitable place. I jumped along the railroad track from tie to tie, and when I came to sections which were too close to villages I crawled along the ground on my stomach, lying quiet when I heard loud Russian voices. I did not want to be arrested again.

After I had gone quite a way I came close to a railroad watchman's house. Curious whether anyone was inside, I slowly crawled close enough to look. The door stood half open. It was all very still. I pressed slowly inside. In the lobby I found the now-familiar scene of destruction left behind by the plundering mercenaries. Then I noticed a strangely sweet odor in the air. It appeared to come out of a room to the side. Entering, I started back in surprise.

Here I saw the proof of that which had been told us so many thousands of times over the radio and in the press. I had almost ceased to believe the reports, realizing that German propaganda was not always true. But here before my eyes was a dead German soldier still recognizable as such by the torn pieces of his uniform. His eyes had been cut out. His fingers were for the greater part cut off. I turned away, shuddering. I got out of there as soon as I could and resumed my flight. I ran into a band of Russians once more but they released me when I showed my paper.

OVERNIGHT REFUGE

I had hoped to reach my home village before the evening, but twilight overtook me. I was only as far as Bartkam, about twelve kilometers from my home. I thought that perhaps it would be best to go into the village. To my joy I discovered a few civilians who greeted me. When I told them my father's name they invited me in to spend the night with them. They set before me a wonderful meal. But when I drew my chair up to the table I got such terribly severe cramps in my legs that everything became black before my eyes; I was suffering from exhaustion. In about four hours I had traveled ten miles along the railroad tracks with a full load on my back. Anybody who has walked on railroad tracks very long and at a very quick pace knows the endurance this feat requires. The women put me to bed immediately and nursed me. Only after I had slept a few hours could I eat anything.

The next morning I got up very early and made myself ready for the homeward journey. The sky and snow were reddened by the first light of the morning. The trees which stood along the way threw long shadows. In the valleys lay a light mist.

To remain undiscovered, I chose a lonely path in the forest. This path was to me perhaps the most beautiful that I had ever taken. Probably because I was returning home, I became more aware of the wonderful beauty of my native landscape. This might be the last time that I would see it for all I knew. In the middle of the forest I stopped before a herd of little deer. They eyed me out of the dark woods with astonishment, looking across as if to ask me why I was in their quiet forest home. Even today I can see the little buck in the front row of the herd, and beside him the sweet doe; it was a picture of deep peace. I stood there very still for several minutes. The deer went further on, grazing slowly. Only when they had gone into the next thicket did I continue on my way.

The forest thickened, then it became thinner, again giving me a free view of the village which lay next to my own home village. At some of the isolated farms I passed, I asked about the Russians. They told me that there were too many around for any peace. I was again forced to make another detour; it was in a very difficult place by the side of the brook where the snow still lay knee-deep. Just before our village lay the corpse of our neighbor's 2,000-pound bull which had been shot by the Russians.

Without any other misfortunes I finally arrived home.

7

FINAL DISPLACEMENT

I do not know how many hours passed until the Russians paid us another visit that day in our temporary quarters in the granary. Everything happened so suddenly. We were all sitting around the hearth. My mother was baking potato pancakes. She was the first one that saw the Russians and told us to hide.

But it was already too late. With quick presence of mind I took the pan in my hand and pretended to be working. *"Heil Hitler!"* mocked the officer and a GPU corporal who was the translator. To our somewhat uneasy answer of "Good day," the corporal shouted at us: "Everyone come along." My younger brothers, fourteen and ten years old, respectively, were left in peace with my mother. My older brother showed his plaster cast and also was released. I was the only one left for them to examine.

I gave my passport to the translator and explained, "I'm sick." In reply they made fun of me and tore up the card. The translator shook me as if I were a scarecrow and the officer boxed my ears. They took me with them when they left. I was unable to prevent my capture. I had to go behind the buggy in which they had come to our village. A group of about ten persons, among them several women, followed behind the buggy.

I was seized by a very strange clammy feeling. It seemed to me that this time all hope was lost. Although the interpreter claimed that we would only be kept for a few days to feed livestock, I did not believe him, nor did I think that I would ever come home again.

But I was most upset about the fact that I had just arrived home at about nine o'clock, the same morning, and now I was being forced to leave at three o'clock that afternoon. I just could not understand why all this had to happen to me. I found out later that this was the last time the Russians came to round civilians up for forced labor in the Soviet Union. If I had been able to hide somewhere, my life would have been considerably different. But on the other hand, maybe God allowed these experiences; I came to the lowest point of my life. Besides a new understanding of the way of God, I became more appreciative of the things I had always taken for granted.

But I didn't know the outcome as I walked silently with the others behind the wagon. I thought about the past and also about the future. What would happen to us? Russian troops continually passed our small group. Most of them were driving new jeeps and army trucks, and on the doors was the inscription, "Made in USA." At least 95 percent of all the Russian military vehicles, with the exception of the horse trailers, traced their origin to North America. Only the guns and much of the other equipment were of Russian origin. When those columns—sometimes miles long—passed us, for the first time I realized that the Germans had been completely outnumbered economically. The proportion was not one to two or one to ten as I had believed, but most of the time it was probably one to a hundred. At that moment I realized that this was the end of our fatherland.

Germany would most certainly be eradicated—ironically, just what Hitler had once promised he would do with other nations.

While we were marching along the road with our minds occupied with thoughts about the future and our miserable present, the interpreter was sitting in the back of the wagon making love to the girls. It was as if we were nonexistent. The main concern was to watch us so that we did not run away. Where could we go anyway? There were Russians all over the place. Previous experience had taught me that it was senseless to risk a walk even when I had written permission.

The sky was cloudy. I felt a little chilly. Both the weather and the surrounding territory depressed me. We came through a village where we saw the remains of three Russian tanks destroyed by bombs. Several German light tanks were also lying in ruins where they had burned out in the field. Once our small troop stopped for the convenience of the guard who wanted to shoot ducks for the evening meal. He shot two and sent me to bring them to the wagon. Finally after we had been marching for several hours we reached the city of Prussian Holland which had been devastated. It was dark by the time we were settled in housing which was still standing there. We men tried to find a place where we could rest our weary legs for the evening; the ladies prepared the ducks for the evening meal. After we had eaten enough of the half-cooked ducks, we slept as well as it was possible under the circumstances. We tried, but it hardly was possible. The Russians were celebrating. As the night progressed, the singing and carousing became louder. Finally, when the Russians became intoxicated from drinking so much vodka, they took the girls from among our number downstairs for the fulfillment of their lusts.

When I awoke in the morning I was more tired than I had been the evening before because I had not slept much. My whole body was completely exhausted. We were forced to make preparations to leave at 7:30 in the morning. Then we were marched through the city and out into the country

65

to the district commander's office. We reached the village during the forenoon and were discharged into a large dance hall of a guesthouse. The door was locked behind us.

I looked around in the room and found a yearly calendar printed in an old newspaper. This calendar later would become my constant companion as well as my diary and date book. Among us prisoners were some German soldiers, part of whom were taken toward the city of Prussian Holland the same day. After their departure we weren't quite as crowded. As a member of the Hitler Youth I had been somewhat prepared for camp life, so I didn't find the situation too bad. But for the women with us, who had slept only on beds since childhood, it was much worse getting adjusted to the hardship.

I prayed to God during the night to graciously undertake for my future. He, after all, was my last remaining confidence in this great sea of disappointments and disillusionments.

"Hunger Cellar"

The next morning the guards awakened us at about 7 o'clock. I shuddered and rolled over, half frozen in the blanket.

"Line up by two's outside and count off!" The translator shouted out instructions. Our entourage began to move in the direction of Prussian Holland. Upon arrival, all the men were locked into a cellar—which was already overcrowded. About three hundred prisoners were jammed in an ordinary house with an average three-room cellar. The women were installed in the upper stories. Among us prisoners were representatives of every group in eastern Germany at that time: soldiers from all sections of the army, civilians from all parts of East and West Prussia, Lithuanians, Estonians, Latvians, and Baltic Germans. Overseeing us were several Poles who treated us severely. The injustice we suffered led us to call our lodgings the "hunger cellar."

Daily we were rationed out about one spoon of half-cooked pea soup. This deprivation was practiced regardless of the fact that most of the people were already out of food. Not everybody had been able to bring food along from home. After my first day there I found a place beside several Lithuanians. These people killed their hunger by putting burning matches into their empty pipes and sucking in the smoke. During the night someone or other always cried for his mother. There were people who became so nervous that if the slightest thing occurred they struck out at anybody who happened to be near them. If anyone still had a slice of bread he could hardly eat it in front of all those people who didn't have anything to eat; if he ate the morsel, many hungry looks were directed toward him. The extreme hunger took away self-control and many acted like animals.

In the "hunger cellar" I met Herbert, one of my former Hitler Youth leaders. After he had successfully evaded the Russians once, they captured him and did not allow him time to pack anything. I tried to help him by giving him a little bread and bacon, and I also gave some to a few other people. But I actually didn't have much, and I had to think at least a little bit about myself. I ate sparingly and rationed out my food as much as possible because I expected worse times to come.

I had picked up the loaf of bread which I had in my possession from an abandoned army bread wagon I saw while we were marching through the woods. By the ruins of the wagon were two German soldiers who had been run over by a Russian tank. Their crushed bodies were frozen; it was a terrible sight.

At this time I sought the company of an elderly man who had been a mason by trade. We took a door off its hinges and laid it on the floor, using it as our bedroom as well as our living room. It was better than sleeping on the cement floor.

For six days we were forced to stay in the cellar. The sticky, unhealthy air passed on death germs to many a man. Undoubtedly this was one of the most unhealthy places I was ever in. The sanitation was also very inadequate. Then the people who had arrived before us were called out. Unemotionally we watched them pass by us, looking like skeletons. What would the future have in store for them? What was going to happen to us under these circumstances? Finally Herbert was called out too. He said good-bye hastily, and that was the last time I saw him.

The exodus of those who were leaving was difficult. While the others tried to make their way out of the crowded quarters, we were pushed around on the inside. During this commotion I lost my cap. The next day I was sorry; when our turn came I had nothing to wear on my head. Since it was quite cold outside I covered my head with a shawl. When the guard called my name I walked over toward the men; but seeing where I was heading, he came after me and directed me to the girls' side. For identification I lifted my shawl; when he saw my haircut, he and the rest of the group had a good laugh about the misunderstanding.

We were taken to another interrogation which was a little rougher than the previous one. When I did not confess to the NKWD officer's charge that I had been in the army, he started to whip me as if I were a juvenile delinquent. I could not prove anything to him but I also could not tell him I was a soldier because I had never been one. I started to weep and tried again to explain my innocence to him. The sorrow on my face was apparently the only thing that moved the Russian. He mumbled something in his beard and said gruffly: "Get out of here."

I was turned over to another guard and locked up in a coal cellar with several other Germans. I tried to level off the coals to make my bed more comfortable; then I lay down and tried to sleep. An elderly man beside me lay groaning from a terrible beating he had received. A Russian police officer had scourged him when he would not confess to the charge that he had been in the Nazi party. His pain must have been intense, for his groanings continued for some time.

68

The methods of capture and the fate of the victims revealed only too clearly the working methods of the NKWD. One forty-year-old farmer reported what transpired during his interview. The interrogating officer asked for the particulars and then wrote the answers down.

Eventually he asked, "Were you ever in the party?"

"No!"

"Don't lie!"

"Really, I never was in the party!"

But when the farmer was searched they found a party emblem in his pocket. For this apparent deception he received a hard beating. The fact that the party emblem had been found on him was recorded in the files and he was marched off with the political suspects.

The farmer told me later that he was manipulated. When the guard pushed him into the interrogation office, the farmer had felt a hand in his pocket. At first he had thought the guard was trying to steal something from him. Later he realized that the guard probably put the party emblem in his pocket by order of the interrogating commissars.

After some time I was removed from these quarters and confined with a few other Germans in the attic of another house in the city. Here, for the first time, bread was given to us prisoners: two slices for each of us. We remained only one night and then we were moved to another room where we stayed another night.

When we awoke the next morning we heard the humming of truck motors and the continual honking of auto horns. Looking through the window, I saw an endless truck caravan parked outside, made up of American army trucks with Russian drivers. Several dozen drivers and guards stood smoking and talking in groups of two or three.

The order was given for us to take our baggage along and leave the attic. We gathered our few belongings together, rolling our blankets and tying them to our rucksacks. Streams of people poured out of the houses of all the surrounding city blocks. Meanwhile, cursing guards with fixed bayonets directed the people to the trucks, and counted them as they climbed in. To each truck they assigned thirty men and one guard.

We had to wait about half an hour before everyone was settled on the trucks. Then the caravan started. In the beginning I didn't know whether I should rejoice or be sorry that we now at last were moving in a definite direction. The only trouble was, no one knew where we were going and what the Russians intended to do with us. The presence of the guard contributed nothing to our well-being. Crows circled the sky.

We moved along well until several trucks had flat tires on the road. When that happened the prisoners from the incapacitated trucks were divided up and added to the still-functioning trucks so that eventually we were pushed together like hogs on a cattle truck. We decided to take turns standing and sitting so that we would be sharing the discomfort. Our journey took us through cities, towns and villages of East and West Prussia which had formerly been flourishing; now they resembled rubbish heaps. The city which had suffered most was Mohrungen, quite famous all over East Prussia because it was the birthplace of the German philosopher John Gottfried von Herder. At dusk we passed through Liebstadt and Gutstadt. Then the night sank down like a dark cloth over the devastated land and faint moonlight illuminated the area. The stillness where there had been so much activity was like death. The hard fighting between the Russians and the Fourth Army had leveled the cities. Few lights were visible, and the former centers of commerce were desolate. It was a terrible scene and an unearthly experience to be passing through what seemed like a ghostland.

IN THE INSTERBURG PRISON

The journey seemed endless. Shivering with cold, I tried to roll up in my topcoat. It was only slight protection against

70

the cold air and the depression of my spirits. We traveled further and further. Toward midnight we arrived at another city, one unknown to me. In the beam of the truck's headlights we saw a big red-brick house with a large gate. Our convoy stopped and we were ordered to get out of the trucks. Apparently we were at the end of our journey. Jumping out, we tried to stretch our legs and arms which had become extremely stiff after fourteen hours of continuous travel. Word was passed along that we had arrived at Insterburg.

After everybody was out of the trucks, we formed a column and then marched into the Insterburg prison, and up quite a few steps into the judgment hall. But, instead of judges, a dozen Soviet officers confronted us. Notes taken at the earlier interrogation and our personal data were piled in big stacks in front of the interpreting officer who read off our names. When my name was called I stepped over to the other side. From time to time a number of people were led away.

A terrible stench filled the hall because many of the prisoners had to perform their necessary bodily functions there, since it was their first chance to relieve themselves in fourteen hours. Although I was afraid at first that the Russians would react badly, it was apparent that they did not seem to mind at all. For them we were merely slaves or animals. As they looked us over, I was reminded of some old slave-catcher stories, for it appeared that each of us was being carefully evaluated according to body constitution, health, and physical fitness. What had happened to the once-so-proud and specially propagated Aryan race? Did this mean its complete destruction? None of us knew what would happen next.

I had secretly hoped that because of my youth the Russians might send me home again. But after they had called all the others without making any exceptions, I realized that there would be no special provision for me. What it would mean to be assigned as a laborer at the age of sixteen to do the same amount of work as any fully grown

71

man I would later find out. With a troop of other civilians I was put into a big, already overcrowded, room located right behind the courtroom. With a bright gleam on his face the guard pushed us into the room and locked the door behind us.

Because of the two or three hundred people in so small an area, the air soon became almost unbearable. Close to the door stood a slop pail we used for a toilet. Its stench penetrated the air. Besides that, it was very hot. I undressed till I had only my swimming trunks on, but I was still sweating. This was a terrible situation, to be able neither to sit nor to lie down and then to sweat as if one were sitting in a Finnish steam bath. A few captured soldiers who were close to the window tried to force it open, but the windows were locked like those in a prison. When the guards in the prison yard noticed the noise they fired a few shots into the air; this action took the wind out of the sails of even the man most zealous to open the window.

When I tried to find a place to sit down, everybody said that there was no room. It was true. There were only legs, luggage and limbs. One could hardly find a place even to stand. Being a newcomer, I tried first to stand for a time. My eyes slowly adjusted to the dark room. Only the reflection of the snow permitted one to see the contours of all the many people, probably close to a thousand, who were huddled together in this hall.

At last I couldn't stand it any longer. I had eaten hardly anything all day. My legs started to shake and the whole hall seemed to turn. I toppled over. But the curses of those on whom I fell and the boot heels of some who kicked at me soon helped me up again and brought me back to reality.

"This is my seat!" shouted one man. "I was here first."

"Don't you have any regard for old age?" fumed another.

"Don't try to sit down here again!" cried a third one.

I was not the only one who didn't have any room to sit down. All those who were constantly shoved into the room through the door were in the same predicament. So

I mumbled an excuse: "Pardon me, but I just can't stand up any longer."

Curses again. I moved on a little to get at least a different position for my aching legs.

NEW FRIENDS

"Watch it," said somebody, "you're stepping on my feet."

I looked down at the man that had just said this.

"He's constantly stepping on somebody's feet," I heard someone else hissing.

"But he needs a place to sit," added the first one again. I noticed from the compassionate undertone of his voice that perhaps at last I might find a place to sit down.

"Move over some," he began again, "and make room for this chap; he needs it." And with this he pushed the two fellows next to him over. They grumbled a bit, but otherwise did what he told them. At last I could sit down. Oh, how good it felt to sit again!

I looked into the outlined face of my benefactor. "Who are you?" I asked.

"My name is Hans." He grinned. Then he went on to say that he was from Succase, close to the Frische Haff, a lake close to the Baltic Sea.

"I know where that is," I answered. "I was there once at a youth retreat when the cherries were blossoming. We went to swim in the lake—that's a very nice place."

"It *was* a very nice place," said Hans. "You should see our village now—gutted by the Russian soldiers."

"Is the farmer of the inn where we stayed still living?" I asked. At his request I told him the man's name.

"Do you see that fellow over there?" he asked, pointing toward the window.

I nodded. "Do you mean the man with the cap on with the mournful and brooding face?"

"That's the one," whispered Hans, as if not to disturb the man who probably couldn't hear us anyway since he was about thirty feet away.

"Well, it's not the same man you knew; he isn't living anymore. That is his brother."

"What happened? Did the Russians shoot him?"

"Yes, under difficult circumstances. They wanted to rape his wife, and he tried to stop them. The Russian raised his pistol and shot him to death, and then they—" Hans stopped. He didn't need to finish the sentence.

We were silent for awhile. This habit of paying homage to our dead countrymen was widely followed.

Later on I asked Hans who the other fellows with him were. He pointed them out separately. Ulrich and Günther; they were sixteen and seventeen years old, respectively, and both were still in high school.

We started to talk about the last days at home, days which had changed our lives more completely than anything else either before or after. Many situations, I learned, were just as bad, and some even worse, than that of my village. The village next to Hans', Dörbeck, had lost about thirty men, mostly farmers. All had been executed.

"Do you have anything along to eat?" Hans asked finally.

"Yes," I answered, honest despite my inclination to lie. "I found a loaf of bread along the road and my mother had given me two pounds of bacon. I've already eaten some of both."

"Great. Perhaps you might give us each a slice of bread and we'll give you some sausage. None of us has any bread; our mothers didn't have any when we were captured."

"OK, it's a deal," I replied. I got out my bread and sliced a few pieces off.

"But I don't even have any sausage to give you," Ulrich admitted.

Hans soothed him: "Don't worry, we won't let you down. We were friends before the Russians came and we still want to be now."

When the bartering was over, Ulrich fumbled in his pocket. After a while he came out with a comb.

"What do you want with that?" Hans laughed at him.

"Oh, perhaps I can give it to Horst; maybe he doesn't have one. I have two anyway."

"You guessed it," I said. "The day they took me for good I had changed trousers and forgot to put my comb into the other pocket. So if you insist, I'll take the comb."

Hans, the natural leader of the group, was tall and erect, with a friendly face. He was seventeen. We soon had finished eating, if one might call it so, for any one of us could have immediately eaten all the food we had left among us. But this symbolic eating together sealed our friendship. We experienced something of that which the disciples of Christ must have shared at the last supper.

More people were pushed into the room. Conditions got more crowded. Curses were hurled from all directions at those who had newly arrived, even though it was obviously not their fault that they were being shoved in with us.

I saw Hans was thinking and after awhile his face brightened. Before long he spoke up with a solution for the problem.

"The space where each of us stands is our own—but let's think of everybody," he announced. "Perhaps we could take turns standing and in that way permit other persons to sit down for awhile."

"Not a bad idea," said Ulrich. "But who shall stand up first? Certainly not me, because I was here first."

"No, this won't work," Hans retorted. "You saw Horst almost falling down on account of exhaustion, so he should be permitted to take his turn last."

Ulrich did not like the idea. But since Kurt felt Hans' suggestion was a good idea and I had no reason to object, it was accepted. In order to convince Ulrich that he himself was not taking advantage of his own suggestion, Hans got up first and stood up for almost an hour.

I tried to stretch out on the floor, but I didn't sleep much that night. By the time I had finally fallen asleep, somebody was shaking me awake. I was almost ready to explode. When a voice said, "It's your turn," I remembered our

75

earlier agreement. I got up to make room for the person who had been standing.

Soon after that the talking ceased. With less activity in the group, the air consumption was decreased. In the middle of the night the Russians brought some food. It was supposed to be divided among all the people, but a few Poles who were lying close to the door took most of it and the people at the other end of the room received nothing. The Russians intentionally favored the Poles rather than the Germans. It was not quite so bad for me not to receive food, as I still had a little bit of bread and about a pound of bacon left.

DIFFERENT QUARTERS

The next day we were put into different quarters on the first floor of another building on the opposite side of the prison yard. This room had a cement floor. Instead of the former exceeding heat, we now had to endure terrific cold. In this room, for the first time in my life, I saw someone become insane because of the horrible treatment. In the middle of the night, as we were trying to get some rest, he started to run around in the room which was completely covered with sleeping people, or at least people who were trying to sleep. He cried with a shrill voice for his mother and demanded to be allowed to go home. He talked like a madman to the guard and stepped on the other comrades' feet; some only retaliated with bad curses but others used their hands or feet to strike him. He was thrown from one side to the other. I felt quite sorry for the man and tried to talk with him, but it did not seem to help, and the Russians continued to have their fun with him. One life did not count much to them.

Then came the third day in prison. At about four o'clock in the afternoon we were driven into a side room with our belongings. We soon found out that this meant baggage control, a favorite Russian trick to seize our belongings in an apparently legal manner. In a little room two young GPU officers were stationed. Each of us was compelled to stand before them and open his baggage. Matches, cigarette lighters, knives, stockings, gloves and other things were thrown on a big pile. Soon after this procedure we had to line up in the prison yard. In this fashion the prison admin·istration had taken its last chance to help themselves to our private belongings before we had to leave. However, the subtle stealing was good for us because now we did not have to carry so much.

The roll was called and we were counted again. One of my good friends, a seventy-eight-year-old farmer from Grosz-Stoboi, was almost unable to walk anymore. He had grown very thin.

"I can't stand this much longer," he said. I tried to console him. To change the subject, I talked about my father whom he knew well.

"Well, where is he now, did they take him too?"

"Yes, they did," I replied. "My mother gave me a sweater for him in case I should meet him in a camp."

"Didn't they give him time to pack a few things?" he inquired.

My answer was an unqualified no.

"But why is he not here with you?" he wanted to know.

"Because the Russians took him on a different day."

Our conversation was interrupted by a guard ordering all of us to form a marching column. We stepped into the ranks. While we stood there, the farmer continued questioning me: "How did it happen?"

I told him. Both of us were deeply affected by the telling.

In the meantime one of the guards ordered us to march after him. I tried to stay close to the old gentleman. But then I felt so thirsty that I decided to get some snow to melt. But I had hardly left the ranks when one of the guards from the rear fired at me. A bullet whisked past me and I stumbled back into the column of the doomed. I had lost the old gentleman. Later I found out that he was one of the first prisoners to die.

LOADED IN BOXCARS

We marched down the road until in the dark we could see the outline of the railroad yard. On the left side of us the silhouette of a long freight train appeared. The guards stopped the column to count us over and then they put fifty prisoners in each boxcar.

Later in the boxcar I felt as if I were dreaming. Click— click—click—the train bustled along the uneven tracks. Click—click—click—each turn of the wheels enlarged the distance from our home. I hated to open my eyes. The empty feeling in my stomach reminded me that I had not eaten anything for several days. In the beginning we had received two slices of toasted bread and an army cup full of water. After that we went for days without being given food or water. Several of the people were ill.

We lay like sardines in the boxcar, beside and on top of each other. No one could stretch out even halfway without resting on the limbs of someone else. When we were pushed into the boxcar, nearly everyone had rushed in to get first chance at the best places. But are there any good places in a boxcar? Since I was one of the last, I sat close to the door with my new friends from the lakeshore.

Some of the soldiers immediately started to make a fire in a little furnace that was there, for it was terribly cold. Tearing off the little boards with which the cracks in the boxcar had been closed, they put them into the small stove. A few matches and paper were produced, and before long the furnace was giving some heat to those hundred outstretched hands.

"Open up!" Someone was madly hammering at the boxcar door. I opened it. Several GPU officers jumped determinatively into the boxcar, making a terrible noise. They turned the stove over, stepped on the feet of those who sat close to the door, and cursed wildly.

78

In a moment's time the fire was extinguished, but the whole wagon was full of smoke. Obviously the Russians did not want us to heat the boxcar in order to keep warm. The officers left again, closing the door, and we were left to suck the smoke into our nostrils. Soon it became cold since the train stood there through half the night. Although I was freezing, I must have fallen asleep. When I awoke again, the train was moving—our final destination a mystery to us.

Click—click—click; the sound filled the cold boxcar but time passed by very slowly. When the sun was shining we tried to determine our traveling direction and the time. Quite a few people still had some food from home, but those supplements became smaller and smaller, especially since many had nothing extra. Sooner or later all of us were forced to get along with the little amount of toasted bread that we started receiving once a day.

DEATH

The cold rays of the eastern sun peered through the cracks of our prison cage and hit my eyes. I tried to avoid them by changing my position. It was still the same. I thought it was strange that the feet on which my head had come to rest did not move. The wheels were still rolling; I could hear the familiar music: click—click—click. The boxcar's bumping irritated me, so I finally decided to pull myself up. I looked at my pillow and found it to be the pale, bloodless legs of my neighbor. My face met his eyes and I murmured something of an excuse to him. But he did not answer. Strange. His eyes looked somewhat past me. *Is he angry?* I thought.

I looked closer, for he lay in the gloomy shadow of the car. There was no movement of the chest, and his eyes looked glassy. A sudden jerk went through my body. Cold moisture crept up my back; I shuddered. I tried to move his legs a little, but they were stiff. Then it dawned on me: I had slept the whole night on this dead prisoner.

79

When the train stopped we waited till the guard passed by. Then we knocked at the door. It was unlocked and the dead body was removed. He was the first person in our car to die. Fourteen more died later.

We passed through the city of Kowno in Lithuania, and from there we went to Smolensk, a city in the southern Ukraine. Our captors, of course, did not identify those cities; but some of the former soldiers among us had formerly been fighting or working in these places and recognized them. From there we turned northward.

THIRST

We underwent terrible overexertion. The hardest physical torture of all was thirst—the one drive which makes the highest demand and is the hardest to satisfy. Although man can live for weeks without food, he can survive without water only a few days. Thirst is a far more intense drive than hunger. When the water supply in the organism becomes low, the organizm must search for water. The tissues of the oil cavity became drier and drier, thus stimulating the tiny nerve endings imbedded in them and producing the consciousness of thirst. We dreamed day and night about water. In my dreams I was compensating for this present water absence. I visualized myself being on a farm and drinking all kinds of juices and drinking as much water as I could. Similar things happened to the others. The thirst was especially hard on us since the toasted bread we were given was completely dry and hard as a brick. Besides that, we received some melted cheese which also could only be consumed with a large supply of water. Thus we chewed the toasted bread in our mouth without any saliva. It felt as if we had sand between our teeth.

Some of the men tried to fish some snow with cooking pans fastened on strings and hung outside through the toilet opening. This procedure worked only if there were snowbanks close beside the railroad track. But the intake was not very big. Often the cooking pans got lost and usually it took hours to get a considerable amount of snow. Then the guards noticed what we were doing and started to shoot at the pots and pans. There were guards stationed in the caboose who could see along the whole length of the train. Only during the nighttime they could not see anything, so some who almost died because of thirst tried to get snow then. The snow water often caused a strong diarrhea so that quite a few more in our boxcar died during the trip. Ulrich became our specialist in snow-fishing.

One night while we were still in Lithuania a shooting began which lasted for quite a while. A Lithuanian had escaped from one of the boxcars. Later we were told that the Russians had been unable to recapture him. Such an attempt was not so hard for him because he was in his home country. Because he had many friends and knew the language and customs of the people, he could more easily slip under cover than the rest of us. For us Germans, escape was a complete impossibility. After this incident the guards ran along the tops of the boxcars each night in order to hinder any escape attempt. We could usually hear them from a distance as they came running from the back, stumbling over our heads, and then running on farther.

For two days the Russians didn't give us any food. The result was not long in coming. When we arrived at Moscow, seven dead men were in our wagon. But this was only the beginning.

8

DESTINATION

Suddenly the train stopped with a jerk. It was evening when the guards opened the boxcar doors and ordered everybody outside with his baggage. Grabbing the few utensils which were left, we jumped out of the boxcar. The below-zero temperature penetrated our bodies which were particularly susceptible to the cold after being confined without any exercise for almost two weeks. Although the boxcar had not been heated, at least our body heat had kept the temperature between 32 and 45 degrees above zero. The snow crunched under our feet and the cutting wind caused pains in the face and on the hands.

After we had lined up, we were ordered to march into a house. Our pitiful-looking column moved slowly into a building close to the railroad depot; it was a bathing establishment. When we came in we rushed toward the furnace to warm up a little. But our leaders soon outlawed this privilege. They told us to get undressed; our clothing was to be disinfected. This was probably necessary since we hadn't had a chance to wash for almost four weeks. The only water we had seen was for drinking and that was insufficient to satisfy our thirst. Only now and then when the train had stopped were we even allowed to wash our hands. Sometimes we were called out for a job like carrying off our dead, and then we did have the chance to wash our hands a little bit in the sub-zero snow. But this could only remove the crust of the accumulated dirt.

We had to take our clothes off and put them on wire hangers; then the articles went into the disinfection furnace. In the meantime we marched to a cement shower room. It was terribly cold; everybody was shaking. We each received a piece of soap about as big as a caramel. But where was the water? No water was coming.

For about two hours we stood there naked in the moist room at a temperature of about 40 degrees above zero. This was especially hard on the elderly people among us, for they were always a little bit more chilly anyway. Many of them caught a cold there which, in combination with the eight-week period of a very insufficient diet, caused them to die soon afterward. We tried to do gymnastics in the shower room, but this was not much of a remedy for the situation since our bare feet were still on the wet floor.

Finally the water came on. Most of us first drank as much as our stomachs could hold before we started to bathe. This was not such a wise idea because the lukewarm water in our empty stomachs caused diarrhea. After the bath we were given our clothing back and were marched outside again. Back into the train we went. Because of the high death rate, many of the individual boxcars had lost quite a few of their inhabitants. Thus we again were divided up fifty by fifty to be put back into different boxcars.

TURN FOR THE WORSE

The train started out slowly. No one suspected that the next segment of our trip to Russia would be the most severe part.

84

One night while the train was stopped at a depot, a band of four drunken soldiers appeared. In order to light up our dark living quarters, they had a pot of oil into which they had put on old rags. This was lighted and used as a lamp. The oil created a terrible stench which was hard on our already dry throats. My tongue lay like a piece of dry wood in my mouth. My palate was sore because of the hard toasted bread, and my stomach felt nauseated. The Russians drove us all to one side of the car and then searched the remaining baggage for useful articles. During this procedure they spilled the rest of the precious water we had saved. Gloves, stockings, belts and other items changed owners again. After they had searched our baggage, they searched us. When I saw that they were not watching, I quickly switched from my side over to the other one where all those who had been already searched were. I was in luck for nobody noticed me. After about half an hour, they left our wagon to carry out the same process in the other boxcars.

Soon after this I contracted a double eye infection, probably because of the continual draft which came in through the inadequately closed door. A soldier named Willy put bandages on me. Now I was blind and felt almost as if my death sentence had already been pronounced. Taking advantage of my sightlessness, someone pushed me over toward the toilet trough. This situation was even more unfavorable because the draft was worse here. If I had not been protected by an old engineer sergeant and my three friends from the Frische Haff, there would not have been much chance for me to stay alive. I was also fortunate that the eye infection did not last too long. It went away without medication or a doctor's treatment. Again I had been spared from possible death.

O God, why all this? I often asked. One misfortune seemed to pile up on the other, and I was miserable.

Meanwhile the train rolled on northward. Once in awhile we stopped briefly in smaller depots. Evidently the Russians did not want us in the southern part of their country. Some of the people told us later that the train officials had tried to discharge us somewhere down south; but since we prisoners were in such bad condition, no one had wanted us. I could understand the truth of that reaction because by then we were a dilapidated crew.

About the time my eye infection was getting better, the guards came around one day to ask for laborers. Our job was to carry the dead. This was the day when I became an unwilling witness to one of the most severe crimes against humanity that I had ever seen. Earlier we had been called out to carry off the dead, and I had helped load the dead corpses into three boxcars which were hitched to the train. They were the death wagons; at that time those special boxcars were not yet full. But when we got there this time, the boxcars were nearly full to the roof. The bodies were lying one beside the other and one on top of the other, most of them with legs or arms stretched out in any position the person had been when he had died, and then frozen stiff. The corpses looked toward us with empty eyes like those of dead fish. It was terrible. But this was not the worst inhumanity.

After we had removed the dead from each boxcar, we were led to a car in the middle of the train. When we opened the door I felt as though my blood had stopped in my veins. It was a terrible sight we beheld: about thirty very sick prisoners had been put into that wagon and left without any medical help, and they had traveled for such a long interval that all of them had died. Bread, wood, and cans of food were lying around untouched. Here was a soldier who had been suddenly caught by death, and there was a woman, her body twisted from the throes of dying. Everything was in a dead calm. The horror of it all rose up at me and I wondered how I had been spared. For I remembered that several days earlier a so-called doctor had come to our boxcar and asked for sick people; all those who had responded had been taken along—apparently to this boxcar!

In my ignorance I had presented myself to that man in the hope of a better fate. But he had not thought my eye infection was serious and had sent me back. Now I thanked God that I was *carrying* the dead and not being carried myself. Why had I been spared other than through divine intervention, I could not understand.

The number of losses by death in our boxcar went up to eight. In the other cars the results were similar or worse. At the beginning the whole transport numbered about three thousand people, but one-fourth, or over seven hundred, died on the way to our actual destination in Russia.

I tried to calculate where we were. Judging by the snow and extremely low temperatures at the end of March, plus our traveling direction, I decided that we must be in the far-northern part of Russia. Of course we were not told where we were, and any conversation with civilians in the short periods we were allowed out of the cars was strictly forbidden.

Arrival at Camp

We stopped once more for an effort at hygiene. After we had been through another bath and a disinfection station, it became obvious that we were approaching our destination. Every once in a while a small group of prisoners was discharged to some camp along the railroad tracks. On both sides of the railroad immense forests stretched across the country as far as the eye could see. Then a depot would appear. I belonged to the last band of prisoners; we were finally discharged.

My three friends and I were close to the door so that it was our lot to jump out first. The snow reached up over our hips. On the little mountaintops around us were guards standing with fixed bayonets and police dogs, ready to dash after us if we attempted to escape. This was our reception committee and our welcome to Siberia.

For weeks we had been in the damp twilight of the boxcar. Now the bright sun above us was hard on our eyes. We were marched through the camp gate into our future dwelling place. Because of eating too much snow once out of the boxcar, my friend Ulrich had become quite ill and exhausted. He had to support himself by leaning on our shoulders. The gate swung shut behind us. We could now see the camp spread out before us; it was composed of log house with wooden shingle roofs. I was put into a comparatively big barrack with a large group.

The guards directed us to the various barracks. About one hundred of us were motioned to the one closest to the gate. My friends and I entered with the other prisoners. The typical prison stench and the twilight of the poorly lighted room were not very inviting. Hardly any daylight filtered through the windows covered by oiled paper instead of glass. We had not quite put our belongings on the wooden bunks when Ulrich rushed out, can in hand.

"Where are you going?" shouted Hans, the tallest of our gang, who was also our undisputed—though never elected—leader.

"I am so thirsty, I want to get some snow," he said hastily and whisked past us.

"Has he regained his strength?" I remarked.

"He could hardly walk when we left the boxcar," said Hans.

By this time our friend had already come back and put his can of snow on the oven.

"Don't you see all that dirt in the snow?" Hans asked.

"Never mind. I've got to drink something. I'm dying of thirst" was Ulrich's almost angry answer.

It took only a few minutes. He grabbed the can of half-melted slush off the stove and sat down on the bunk. Pulling out his spoon, he started to eat.

"Couldn't you have waited a little till it was all melted—and then boil the water?" Hans pleaded.

"Who appointed you to be my guardian?"

Hans saw it was useless to argue further.

Soon after he had eaten, Ulrich's condition became so bad

that he had to be moved, together with some others, to the hospital. It was a whitewashed building made of wooden planks which was certainly no place to recuperate. Rats and gnats populated the building and its surroundings. The meals as well as the beds and treatment were all inadequate. Our friend suffered from dysentery, only partially brought on by his indulgence for dirty snow.

The next day when I happened to be walking across the camp yard, I saw Ulrich again. He was dead. His naked body lay on a *panjesled* (Russian sled) ready to be moved to the storehouse where it would be left until there were enough other bodies so that it would be worthwhile to dig a grave. Till that time, death had been rather impersonal because I had not known any of the people too well. This time it was a good friend.

I understood better as time went on what had happened to Ulrich's clothes. The Russian hospital attendants had stolen them after he died. At a later date they would be sold on the black market. German clothes were in much demand among Russian civilians.

Two Catholic priests were with our group, one of whom was mortally ill. It was a heartrending scene when the younger priest gave holy communion to the older one before he closed his eyes forever. I was well aware, as were others, that truly God and belief in Him were all that could help us in these moments. But I wonder now if we really believed in Him as more than an idea. Hardly anyone confessed Jesus Christ as a personal being. Christians we were in name only. As for myself, I had been confirmed, but never had come into the presence of the living Christ and been born again. Nor had I ever made much a profession of being a Christian. But now I and the other men were helpless, committed to this uncertain future. No longer could we cope with life in our own strength. If ever we had needed God, it was now; on that we all agreed. Most of us had built on a different foundation. All those other foundations had been swept away. Was there something better we could have built on?

At least in the camp we received regular meals. The food served to us consisted of cabbage (the green, slimy, putrid outside leaves which were left after the white ones had been sold to the Russians), turnips, moist bread (often baked from cornmeal), and *kasha* (cereals which were cooked in a porridge). Besides these staples we received a very salty codfish which led many to drink much water, which in turn often brought on a sure death. We received so little meat and oil in our diet that even with a microscope it would have been hard to find them. All of this food was doled out in very limited quantities. Because of the near-starvation diet and the radical change of climate, many men could not survive. The gradual drainage of strength from all these hardships caused many premature deaths.

CAMP LIFE

Four main sicknesses took a daily toll. First was cholera, which caused a continual diarrhea which weakened the body to such an extent that the prisoners died of it very soon. Dropsy caused the joints to swell until finally they became so stiff that it was painful to walk. Almost everybody who had this disease had a water belly and a swollen face. The water rose from the bottom of the feet higher and higher until it finally reached the area of the heart, and after that death was certain. The third sickness was influenza with a high fever. The fourth scourge was general physical exhaustion because of overexertion and complete inadequacy of food.

For these four illnesses there were specific drugs given by the camp guards; we called them whiskies because they were given to us in whisky glasses. All of these so-called medications tasted alike but they came in different colors. Against cholera they also gave us charcoal tablets.

Offhand I would say that 50 percent of the deaths could be traced to inadequate medical care, and 50 percent to inadequate food. It seemed as if there must have been a clause in Soviet headquarters which approved the death of prisoners in large quantities. As a rule the doctors had not studied medicine any longer than two semesters. Sometimes they couldn't even fix a good bandage, not to mention their lack of knowledge on how to keep really sick people alive. Depending on their degree of hatred against the prisoners— especially the Germans—they took greater or lesser pains in looking after them. At times our daily death rate out of forty to fifty hospitalized prisoners was five to seven. The whole camp population was around three hundred.

In the beginning the hospitalized received the same kind of food given to the healthy prisoners. The doctors had been advised by the camp administration to excuse as few as possible from work, so even among the so-called healthy ones, a large percentage were sick. Besides that, the officials soon recognized that our German civilian clothes were of better quality than their own, which were drab and quilted. Accordingly, when someone died he was always stripped of his clothes. For this reason the Russians were not too interested in the recovery of the sick prisoners. On the contrary, they had more to gain by a prisoner's death. Since the administrators had already established such a flourishing business with the clothes of the dead, they depended on the constant death of more prisoners to keep the business going. There were even customers among the civilians outside the fence who paid a high price for those clothes. Sometimes they could not even wait until a poor soul had drawn his last breath on earth before removing his clothes.

After our arrival at the camp the officials told us that we would get ten rest days so that we might recover from the death ride we had just endured, and be ready for work. This promise was never realized. In a few days it was Easter and we were forced to start working. I couldn't figure out whether the Soviets made us start working during the Easter holidays because they didn't recognize the Christian holidays anymore or because they knew that Easter is the day Christians commemorate the rising of Jesus Christ. At any rate, we were quite disgusted because the promise had not been kept. Furthermore, because of hunger, our bodies were so emaciated and stiff that no one wanted to move around much.

The only decent thing that occurred in those days was the fact that we received new work clothes (a quilted coat, trousers and a set of linen underwear) without being required to turn in our own clothing. In the new work outfits we easily could be mistaken for Russians, for we had been given butch haircuts some time ago.

WORK BRIGADES

The camp was divided into working brigades. The leaders were Poles for the most part. In spite of the fact that we were all prisoners, their hatred of us Germans was even stronger than that of the Russians.

Membership in the different brigades was delegated according to age, height and general health conditions. The Russians lumped every human being into certain categories just like animals. The first and second categories, which were composed of the healthiest people, had to do the hardest work. The third category was composed of people who were not quite so strong. They usually did easier jobs which were bad enough in themselves. The fourth, the OK (or better, KO, standing for "knocked-out") brigade, was composed of people who were weak, halfsick, or just discharged from the hospital. This brigade of convalescents was used to do certain jobs without any set norms. The women received complete equality in the sense that they had to do the same jobs as the men; this too is a method of Russian socialistic progress.

In the beginning I was classified in the third category. Our brigadier was a twenty-year-old Pole who had worked for a baker in Elbing and who, for some reason, did not like me. After that I was fortunate in that I was transferred to the OK brigade. The Pole, because of his inadequacy as a leader, was soon put as a worker into another brigade.

92

Our jobs in the OK brigade were sawing wood, carrying water, and shoveling snow. My companion in sawing was usually the young Catholic priest; he soon became my friend. I was sorry that later on we were separated when, after his hospitalization, he with other sick prisoners was transferred to another camp. Incidentally, the Russians had stolen his deceased colleague's rosary.

During the time I spent in the OK brigade I recovered, so one day I was suddenly transferred to the third category again. Our new brigadier was a German-Pole; he was born a German in West-Prussia, but when his province became Polish territory after World War I, he became a Polish teacher and an officer in the Polish army. In 1939 after the occupation of Poland he again quickly switched to the Volks-German camp. Because of his excellent knowledge of the Russian language he had become the camp commander of a Russian POW camp in the vicinity of Elbing. After the occupation of the city by the Russians in 1945, he again changed his mind and once more became a Pole. The Russians had arrested him, accusing him of mistreating the Russian prisoners in that camp.

Like all the others, our working brigade was composed of twenty-five to thirty people. The brigadier was responsible for the performance of any given job, but he did not work himself. He watched closely to see that the job was done technically right. A work norm for the whole camp was established by a *Normerowchick,* who was a Volga-German, part of a German minority who had settled around the Volga River in the eighteenth century. The work of all the brigades was supervised by a work chief. Military guards were supplied by the GPU, and above all of them was the *Natchaillnic,* the camp commander, who was usually a first or second lieutenant of the GPU. Besides that, a whole mass of other employees were at the camp: bookkeepers, interpreters, a disinfection chief who was responsible for exterminating pests in our dwellings, a cook and a doctor. These personnel were of course our superiors too. The interpreter of our camp was Hellwig, a Volga-German, as was the chief of the foodstuffs, Theisz.

CAMP HISTORY

Our camp had been built by Polish soldiers in 1939. They had been forced to build a railroad to Vorkuta, a coal and oil district close to the Ice Sea. The coal found there is mixed with slate and is of low quality. It is shipped down to Leningrad, where it is used for processing iron ore. About 6 percent of Russia's coal comes from there. Our camp was located close to the Ishma River, a tributary of the Petchorra River.

The territory in which our camp was located is called the Socialistic Komi Republic (Komi-SSR); originally it was inhabited by the Komi people, nomads who are closely related to the Lapps in northern Finland. Only once did I see a band of ten of these people riding to the Ishmar market in their colorful clothes, somewhat resembling those of Eskimos.

Also located in the Komi-SSR close to the women's camp, *Solwitche Gorsk*, there was from earlier times a tower; in it Stalin supposedly was kept prisoner prior to the Communistic revolution. When he became the head of the USSR it is claimed that he said: "Since I was banned once to that territory, from now on all those who will be banned by me shall go there!" And, as far as we knew, he translated his words into deeds. The Komi-SSR became a criminal colony of the USSR, with the only contradiction being that not all those brought there were criminals in the true sense of the word. The Russian prisoners and even the guards and camp administrators usually had done something for which they had to suffer here, be it in a political or a general way. However, the crime of most of the foreign prisoners was that they simply had not been born in Russia. Our crime was that we were Germans.

Besides the hospital, there were three women's brigades,

three men's brigades and the OK brigade in our camp. At first my brigade was used for earthmoving jobs. Later on we were sent to do a special job. About one and a half miles from the camp was a great sandpile which had been worked on by a steam shovel. The sand was used to build railroad fills. Almost everything in that part of Russia was connected with the railroad; it was the life stream of the country.

Our Work Assignment

Railroad tracks had been laid close to the steam shovel so that the trains could come nearby to be loaded with sand. It usually took the steam shovel about a month to load the sand piled on a stretch of land thirty feet wide and one-third mile long. Then we had to move the railroad tracks close to the steam shovel again for further loading.

We had other responsibilities, such as keeping up the tracks and building switches. The biggest problem, however, was to keep the steam shovel supplied with wood, for it was not propelled by a motor but was a steam shovel in the truest sense of the word.

In spring and fall when the ground was frozen rather hard, we had to drill blast holes with heated iron bars which we hammered into the ground. Any trees growing on the hill and any moss covering it had to be removed too, for the gravel was supposed to be free of any organic material which would later rot and cause the railroad fill to sink.

The work was directed by a Russian, a former prisoner who had been paroled but was required to serve the rest of his term in that territory. A comparatively just boss, he tried to understand our situation even though he did not know a single word of German.

Hardest for all of us was the fulfillment of the high standards of work. Whether it was moving moss, putting together tracks or sawing wood, a norm was established for everything. I always marveled that the Russians were able

95

to reach comparatively high goals with the most primitive tools and means.

For instance, stretching out or putting together rails which were too short or too long was one of their specialties. For this purpose their *only* tool was a thirty-yard-long rail which was used as a sledge hammer moved by human hands; it was jerked against the other rails till they fit.

On the other hand, there was a noticeably short lifespan of the work of our labors and a quick disintegration of everything. The products which had been made by human hands lacked the precision and the good raw material which make for lasting quality. Everything was to be done in record time, and how it was done didn't matter. Everybody was required to meet his norm. How the job was done was not always unimportant; nevertheless, often it was not too important either.

Within half a year six railway carriages and one steam engine were derailed. All had fallen between the rails which gave way under pressure. This happened because we had to use the same wooden ties over and over again. And the nails which were supposed to hold the rails in place had to be driven into the same holes that had been used before. Therefore, it wasn't surprising that the rails could not support the train. However, the derailed steam engine was pulled out in a remarkably short time with another engine. Even though much of this experimentation was extremely unsafe, very seldom did anything happen to harm the working men.

A Day in Camp

Our daily camp routine was monotonous. At six A.M. we were awakened by a guard pounding a hammer against a piece of rail. After we had washed and dressed and had received our meal in the dining room, the brigadier went to the bread master to receive two hundred grams of bread for each prisoner and divided it among us. The bread-cutting job and the weighing of the portions were special duties carried out by a trustworthy Russian whose job was to cut the portions three times daily. The small pieces were usually fastened to the ration with toothpicks.

The cook dished the soup out, with several German girls serving. The prisoners received 500 grams of water soup and 200 grams of porridge; the brigadier received double rations.

Soon after the meal we were marched to the gate of the camp, where we were ritually counted. Behind the gate we were transferred to another guard. It was his duty to remind us that he would make use of his gun if we disobeyed his orders. The brigadier translated the words of the guard into German. After that, all of us were required to answer in the Russian language, "We understand." Then we marched away.

At our working place we were received by the master who explained the job to the brigadier. If we were at the same working place as before, one of the first things to do was to start a fire for the guard. In carrying out this job we had to be very careful to maintain the required three-yard distance from the guard. When bringing wood for his fire, we had to lay it on the ground three yards away from him. Then the guard himself put the wood on the fire. One fire was made for our group of twenty-five men, and obviously it did little to warm us all.

During that time I thought a great deal. The Latin proverb which was engraved on the Elbing courthouse often came to mind: *Suum quique*—"To everybody his own." I wondered if everybody received what he deserved. Was this prison experience the humiliation intended for us by God? Even though God was impersonal to me, I didn't want to blame Him for my situation. But I saw no solution to my plight.

Dinner was brought to the working place, and after eating we worked until five or six o'clock in the evening. Shortly before quitting time we often had to do a different type of job so that our master could record additional work for us. Although we never did accomplish much as far as quantity was concerned, the main thing was that our master could write something else on his daily work report which he handed in each night. Thus it appeared to the administration that we had really accomplished much more work than we actually had. Our master did this out of compassion for us so that we might receive more bread. Our remuneration was based on the work carried out that was reported to the office.

At the end of our long day we marched two by two home to the camp, the guard behind us.

Often I walked with Mr. Kaufmann, a baker from Elbing. He was about fifty-four years old and had seen more of the world than any of us. In World War I he had been wounded in one leg, so he limped a little, but in general he was a good worker. During the First World War he had also been a prisoner, that time in England. While walking back, I asked him: "Where would you rather be in prison—in England or in Russia?"

"That's not hard to answer," he replied. "I would much rather be in an English camp. The treatment was far better there than what we are getting here. But there's another choice which you didn't mention."

"What's that?" I asked curiously, shifting my saw from one shoulder to the other.

"I would rather be caught by the Americans," he confessed. "They usually treat their prisoners best."

"How do you know?"

"Oh, I had a distant relative who was caught in Italy in 1944. He wrote from the States that he received fried chicken when he arrived in New York."

"Fried chicken! Will we ever have that again?"

"If Hitler had not agitated the Jews and the Americans, he might even have won the war, and we never would have been sent here."

"Not a bad idea," I observed, "but how could he have done it?"

Kaufmann didn't have to think over that answer. He had already made up his mind.

"If we had borrowed more money from the U.S. and let the Jews lead the life of normal citizens, then America would have remained our friend. And perhaps if Hitler would have conducted a more moderate foreign policy, we still would be at home."

Meanwhile we had reached camp. The guard had already opened the gate for us. We put down our tools, shook the dust from our clothes, and marched into the camp compound. Again the gate swung shut. Another guard counted us over. The length of this procedure depended on the IQ of the guard in charge.

We all were there. What good would it do for us to leave? There was nowhere to go. Then we had the evening meal with the usual rations, plus the reward of extra rations for the fast workers. The quality of the bread was very low. The dough contained so much water that it had to be baked in molds to keep it from running away. Leaven was used in large quantities so that the bread might be thoroughly baked despite its high water content. This produced much indigestion.

Six hundred grams of bread was the portion given to the hospitalized, the sick, and the maintenance men; seven hundred and fifty grams went to the working men who did not reach their norm; eight hundred grams were given to the brigadier; for those who reached their norm, nine hundred grams were allotted. Sometimes we received cold cereal cakes called *Sabikanntka*. Even though these rations might not appear to be very low, every prisoner of the Russians would testify that none of the prisoners found that the meals satisfied their appetites because all the food was low in calories. Even after eating, any one of us would have been able to eat two pounds of bread.

Our daily routine closed with the evening bell. Every prisoner had a very simple wooden bed. Part of his clothes he used to cover himself and the rest served as a mattress. Since it was cold and extremely uncomfortable, the sleep we were allowed was not too refreshing. And because of the excessive water which we all drank in order to fill our empty stomachs, we were forced to get up frequently during the night, sometimes as many as nine times. Our exhausted bodies did not get much rest, and dawn often found us more weary than we had been the previous evening. This was an average day. Exceptions were when we were called out during the night to help get derailed cars on the track again.

Our work at the sand hill was not categorized as hard work and therefore we had lower rations. Even so, we discovered the hard labor which was necessary to carry water-soaked railroad ties and thirty-yard rails. Many of my companions were the same age as I, only sixteen or seventeen. We had to do the same work as thirty-year-old laborers who were accustomed to the strenuous labor through years of work.

Other camp brigades did shoveling, made necessary by the uneven terrain. In the hasty building of the railroad, the engineers had adjusted the railroad fill to follow the rolling landscape. This was actually contrary to good engineering principles since a railroad can only reach its highest efficiency if there are few grades.

The Izhma River passed near our camp; it had a very steep bank. On both sides of the river were high hills which were hard for the trains to cross. The other prisoners had to put in a new fill beside the old railroad fill to overcome its steepness. Thousands and thousands of cubic yards of dirt had to be wheeled up on wheelbarrows by German men and women.

Rising Work Norm

The work norm continually rose and the starving people were bribed with special rations to get the last bit of energy out of them. Everybody worked harder and harder to get a little more to eat. They worked with only one idea in mind: *Today I'll break my own record.* In so doing, the workers exerted themselves to the limit of their capacity. In the beginning only a few reached the norm; then more did; and when about half of the workers had finally made it, the norm was set higher. With only a few ounces of bread in our stomachs, we prisoners were driven on to goals almost humanly impossible.

Then the only thing that stopped their effort was an over-worked heart which refused to cooperate further, and death resulted. It was especially in those days that I began to meditate about the mystery of immortality. If I should succumb and leave this life, what was beyond? Now I pondered in all seriousness if there was a God who heard the prayer of His children. My prison life was like a Babylonian captivity. Could He deliver me?

One after the other of my brigade went to the *lazarette* (hospital), some never to return. One after the other went to the graveyard, where no cross nor flower marked their graves. Only a number identified the burial plot, and it was not always the same personal identification number as that recorded in the files of the administration. Hundreds of thousands were buried in the tundra of Russia. At home they were merely recorded as missing. No effort at accuracy was made. Many loved ones waited years in the hope of their survival, but many waited in vain.

As more and more of our men, women, boys and girls were continually caught by death—comrades with whom one had pulled on the same saw the day before—with a little shrug of your shoulder you silently asked yourself the question, *Will I be next?* In the beginning I was often affected by the proximity of death, but I soon became accustomed to it, along with the other deprivations.

Our treatment was inexcusable for human beings but justified in the Russian mind for several reasons. I believe that the Russians were interested in the destruction of the German people at large, and that they wanted working material which could be used regardless of loss.

Such utter disregard by our captors for the dignity of human beings was an attitude I ranked as the worst of crimes. My feelings toward the Russians because of this action were very bitter. I discredited the Russians as a race. Such treatment, I believed, would never be perpetuated by my nation—Germany.

9

HUMAN EXPENDABILITY

The days passed monotonously until one day in spring. It was cold and rainy and our clothes were soaking wet. No one was ever excused because of bad weather; we went on with our work of carrying rails. That day quite a few had stayed home on account of sickness, and there were only about fifteen or eighteen in our brigade. We walked over to the tracks to pick up a rail. I was next to Werner, a young, quiet lad from one of the villages in East Prussia. Together we lifted the rail but it did not come off the ground. Looking over at Werner, I saw that he was hardly lifting. Because of the added weight, my back was aching.

"Why don't you lift your part?" I asked him.

"I can't anymore," he muttered.

"I think you're just pretending," I replied angrily.

"I wish I could have stayed at home," he answered, almost weeping. "The doctor wouldn't let me stay home. He felt just the same way you do."

He had turned his face toward me with an accusing look. I saw his running nose, his reddened eyes, and his worn-out facial expression.

Then the guard swore angrily at us and yelled orders to pick up the assigned rail.

We made a final effort and up came the rail. We had started walking the fifty yards over to the place where the new tracks were being built when Werner stumbled behind me. Suddenly he fell.

Someone shouted: "He's only pretending; all of us are just as sick as he is."

"He isn't faking," I shouted back, "I know it."

"Then he should have stayed at home," cried another one.

"Should have," I heard Hans say. "Did you ever try to stay in the barracks against the doctor's will?"

We finally reached the place where the rail was to be installed. By this time we were puffing in exhaustion. Hans lifted the hammer and started to nail the rail in place. He was really a specialist at that, hardly ever missing the nail's head. Werner came walking behind. The guard cursed at him but Werner seemed too weak to even reply.

Finally it was about twelve o'clock. Dinner was brought by two Russians from the camp and the brigadier handed out the rations. Some were smaller; apparently the two carriers had cut something off. The brigadier gave the bigger rations to the better workers and the smaller rations to the poorer ones. Werner was among the latter. By now he was shivering. The healthier fellows sat closest to the fire and Werner was unable to get closer. He lacked the fighting strength.

So Hans said, "Why don't we all move out a little and make room for Werner?" The workers reluctantly complied, even though it was obvious by now that Werner was not pretending. The wind blew and sparks from the fire flew around. Someone put a new piece of wood on the fire and started more sparks flying into the air. Suddenly we smelled something like burning cotton. I looked around and saw that

Werner's coat had caught fire. It was not burning, but smoldering. I caught him by the arm and shouted, "Quick, get up! You're on fire!"

"I don't care. It's no use anyway."

Hans had already jumped to his feet and started to unbutton Werner's coat. Werner put up little resistance but gave no assistance either. Hans tore Werner's coat off and dipped it into the water. There was a hole as big as a hand but it stopped burning. Werner put his coat on and slowly buttoned it up again.

"You're just a lazy crank," said the brigadier. "The guard is really angry about you."

"Let him be, who cares," Werner replied weakly. "All I'm longing for is to go home to be with my mother; she would understand me."

"You're a real baby. Do you want a baby bottle?" the brigadier asked sarcastically.

Werner didn't say anything anymore. There was no use. The brigadier told us to get up and start working again. Werner got up too. He wanted to go back home but the camp was about two miles away.

"Where are you going?" shouted the guard.

"I want to go home to my mother," Werner replied.

"Do you want to get shot?" shouted the brigadier.

"I wouldn't care, I am through with this world." The guard readied his gun. We held Werner back.

Finally the brigadier spoke: "OK, you don't need to work this afternoon. But don't you dare go home. You know that none of us are allowed anywhere without a guard."

Werner was resigned now. He turned around and sat down close to the fire. He had it all to himself. Most of the wood was burned down and only a few damp branches were still smoldering.

We worked on the rails and ties till evening. The air was even more chilly later on in the day. From the distance we could see Werner huddled by the fire. Finally we were permitted to go home. We shouldered our tools and fell in line. The brigadier shouted for Werner but he did not come. Then the brigadier motioned for two men to go after Werner. They had to lift him up; his face was blue and he couldn't walk anymore. Two more volunteered to help carry Werner and others took along the extra tools he usually carried.

We trotted home, past the old boxcar in which our foremen lived, and down the tracks. A train was whistling and we stepped off the tracks because it had the right of way. After a little over half an hour we reached the camp. Werner was taken to the hospital. We sat down and pulled off our wet clothes. We had spare clothing to change into; everybody stood close to the stove to catch a little heat. Warmth meant the difference between survival and death at this point.

There was not much talk after supper. Some of us had taken part of our bread along to the barracks. We all knew that we would be too hungry to fall asleep if we didn't eat something before going to bed.

Suddenly Hans came rushing in. "Quick, does any of you have any bread left over? Werner is dying."

Several of us contributed a piece of bread. We hurried over to the hospital barracks with the food. There were about thirty in the hospital room with Werner. Several had died that day but their bunks were already filled with new candidates for death row. The odor of a poorly ventilated room intermingled with the usual medicinal smell of the hospital was awful.

We walked over to Werner's bed. When he saw us he asked in a hardly recognizable voice, "Where is my mother? She has something for me. Apples, oranges, bananas and juice. That will make me well."

I looked at Hans. We understood each other. There was no use telling him that his mother was a thousand or two thousand miles away.

"Do you want some bread?" asked Hans in a gentle voice.

Werner jerked himself up. "I don't want bread. I sent Mother to fetch some oranges."

None of us had seen any oranges for almost two years. So Hans said, "Perhaps you should take some bread until your mother brings the oranges. Here's something to drink."

"You are a good boy, Hans. You helped me out there at the tracks. Perhaps I will eat a little bread."

We all stretched our hands out. He took a little piece of bread from the nearest and drank a little water. Once more his face brightened, but it had a strange look. Werner started to shake, and then his strength seemed to leave him. He fell down on his bunk. We knew it was the end. Soon each of us started to move our chapped hands, folding them in prayer for a soul approaching eternity. It was all that we could do.

We stood there in reverent silence. The reprimands of a Russian orderly told us to leave: "There are no visiting hours now!" We knew what it meant. Others had told us. He was after Werner's clothes.

The death of Werner was only another grisly event in this joyless existence of ours.

RECREATION

Occasionally we were permitted some recreation. Twice we were allowed to go to the movies in the town of Ishmar which was five miles away. This was supposed to be a special reward for extraordinary achievements in the accomplishment of the work project. We learned later that the Russian camp administration had used up the money which had been sent to us as compensation. The trip to the movies was an effort to show us at least some appreciation for the work we had done. They had bought themselves an easy living at the cost of the lives of hundreds of people. This was not an example of social justice but rather of personal gain. The content of the films was mostly of a political nature so we did not enjoy it much. One of them pictured the outbreak of the Russian October Revolution and the reign of Kerenskij, the first president after the revolution. Stalin was shown on his flight in 1917 from the territory we were now living in. The second film showed the struggle and final victory of the guerillas over the German army. I considered this as horrible baseness, to show us these films in the presence of the Russian population who didn't think much of us anyway.

GERMANY SURRENDERS

One morning when we were all lined up at the camp gate, the Russians stood at attention in a particularly ceremonial posture. Something extra was in the air. The interpreter was reading something in Russian which he translated into German.

"The German army has surrendered!"

The translation was for us only a confirmation of long-expected events. We did no work that day. It was a rest day, and this was in a sense something special. In Communistic Russia the worker only gets every tenth day off. This decimal system of working hours is also an achievement of the revolution. The people are thus forced away from God and His seventh day of rest. The same method was tried during the French Revolution without success. In a sense this extra holiday was for us something like the funeral of the Third Reich, and we helped to celebrate it. Later on one day was subtracted from our holidays, so in the end we had gained nothing.

Many prisoners in our camp were women and girls. For them, camp life was even more difficult. On a nice summer evening I happened to walk across the camp yard. A number of girls sat chatting in front of the adjoining barracks. How unlike the girls back home they looked! Their long hair had been completely shorn off to keep out the lice. Instead of light summer dresses, they wore quilted jackets.

"If I were at home now," reflected one, "I would eat an apple or drink some cider."

"We used to have so many strawberries," another cut in. "Oh, was that ever a treat, eating those berries while picking them for market."

"Yes," said a third girl, "my mother used to prepare them with sugar and whipped cream."

It was one of the usual escapes of these poor creatures, to think about home and food. Most of them had hardly ever left home before. They were used to hard work, but not to pushing wheelbarrows all day.

FAMILIAR FACE

I stopped and listened to their conversation. They fell silent. One of them was a woman about twenty-three years old; she regarded me intently. After awhile she asked: "Haven't I seen you before? Your face looks familiar. Where are you from?"

"I am from Neuendorf-Höhe in the county of Elbing."

"I am from Serpin! Then we are almost neighbors." She smiled at the irony of our position.

"What is your name?" I wanted to know more about her.

"My name is Hube."

"Hube?" I reflected over her name. "We had a girl working for us on the farm who was called Hube. She was from Serpin."

She grinned. "That was my sister. Is your name Otto-Karl or Horst Gerlach?"

"My name is Horst. Otto-Karl is an older brother of mine. The GPU left him at home because he had a broken leg."

We had a type of reunion. She was the first person in the camp whom I had known before. We exchanged some of our camp experiences, and I found she had been in the women's camp and had just lately arrived at this camp.

When it became late we finally parted. "In case you have anything to mend, just bring it over," she said. "I can do it for you, since you don't have your mother here. She was always so good to my sister."

I blushed. "Really it is not necessary, I—"

"Come on," she insisted. "I'll be glad to do it for you."

"OK, but I really don't have anything now that needs mending."

109

"All right, then, good night!" She smiled and went with the others into her barrack. I went to ours. As I undressed and unfolded my blanket, I held it up to the lamp. The rays of light fell on my face. I knew I had not told the truth when I said nothing of mine needed mending.

When the next rest day came I took heart and went over to her with my blanket. She sat on her bunk like most of the thirty other girls and women in the barrack.

"Did you find something that needs mending?" She beamed.

"Of course I did," I replied, "and I would like to apologize."

"That's all right, never mind." So we sat and chatted while she patched the blanket.

A few weeks later we stood in front of the guardhouse, ready to march to our project. When I looked over at the women's brigade, I saw a thirteen-year-old-girl, the youngest of our camp; somehow she had survived. But Miss Hube was not there.

"Where is she?" I inquired of Mrs. Brettschneider, the woman brigadier.

"Did you not hear, she was taken to the hospital," answered Mrs. Brettschneider quickly. The guard was motioning her to lead her brigade out of the camp.

"What's the matter with her?" I called after the brigadier.

"The usual thing—dropsy. Go and see her. But I must go now."

I knew what dropsy meant. Our chamber attendant, a healthy fellow from Poland, had come down with swollen legs and a swollen face. Three days were spent in the hospital and then he was dead. One of the soldiers who had withstood the strain of six years of war, most of the time in Russia, also contacted dropsy. One day he was sitting in front of the hospital in the warm sun of June when he suffered a fatal heart attack. He was not even thirty.

When evening came, I went to the hospital. Miss Hube

110

was talking to a girl on the next bunk. In their talk they were cooking again. When she saw me, she smiled but her face showed strain. "Here are your gloves, Horst, I mended them for you," she said.

"Well, thanks a lot, but I don't need them now. It's summer."

"That's right." She sighed. "I don't know if I will live to see the next winter."

"Come on, you'll make it. Get some rest here and then you will be well again."

"You know how many they carried out of here this morning?" the neighboring girl pitched in.

"No, I have no idea."

"Well, this morning three were dead. The other day we had four. We are twenty in here." She sank back on her bunk.

I looked at Miss Hube. "But you will get better."

She sighed. "I don't know. I can't push those wheelbarrows anymore. The other day I didn't feel well, but the doctor wouldn't let me stay home."

We talked some more about the doctor and camp life. When I left she said, "Wait a moment, here is my bread ration. I couldn't eat it today."

I wanted to refuse it although I felt hungry. After much urging I finally took it. When I left I had the strange feeling that she might not make it.

A few days later another girl met me on the camp grounds and gave me a message. I was supposed to go to the women's hospital. I did not need to ask any questions; I went right away.

When I looked at Miss Hube's bunk, another face was there. The girl who had slept next to her smiled weakly at me and then whispered:

"Before she died, she said, 'Give this bread to Horst. I won't need it anymore.' She had saved the rations of several days." With that she motioned to her pillow. There were

about four pounds of bread, some already moldy. We talked
a bit more about our dead friend before I went home. I gave
Hans and the others some of the bread. We were glad for an
extra ration, but knowing the reason we had it spoiled our
appetites. I could not eat any that evening. The meaning
and implications of death were too strong and they did not
leave me for some time.

ADDED FREEDOM

Interrogations and investigations were continued all summer; we were used to having them frequently. When one
was conducted, certain prisoners were asked to stay at home.
Then the NKWD came. In contrast to the haggard look of
the prisoners, they appeared well-fed and wore excellent
uniforms with blue rank badges. When a prisoner was called in, usually he was first asked casual questions to make
him feel more at home. Then came the tougher ones. We
soon realized that often they asked the very same questions
other interrogation officers had asked at our first appearance
before them. Our files followed us. All the answers were
written down and compared. What they were after was to
find out whether the prisoner ever contradicted himself.

A man who had been in the SS or another special unit and
had lied about it might have been betrayed in the meantime by an anti-Fascist, usually a prisoner who had been won
to the Communist cause and was tempted by higher rations
to repeat casual remarks made by a fellow prisoner. In the
NKWD vocabulary, *crimes*, or war crimes, in addition to the
usual meaning of the term, meant butchering a Russian hog,
employing Russian prisoners, or permitting a German army
horse to graze on a Russian meadow. As young men, our
cases were not too complicated because our age had not
permitted us to be either soldiers, party members or
members of the SS—a group which became a criminal
organization.

But those above eighteen years of age, whose unit might
have been stationed in Russia, had an especially difficult

time. If anything negative about the unit came to the attention of the interrogators, they were in for trouble. So were those who had been only nominal members of the Nazi party. Those who really had committed crimes had been eliminated before this questioning, and others had died or else fallen into the hands of the Western powers. So during the three or four days the NKWD was in camp, the ones in question had nightmares about what they might be asked or what right or wrong things might be said.

On August 25, 1945, all the captive soldiers were called out and moved away. None of us knew where they went. Certainly there was no idea about repatriation. Where would they have to go? No one knew anything for certain, except that they would be taken to another camp and be guarded more heavily.

Among those who were moved on September 6, 1945, was our brigadier, Urban. Because of his excessive use of tobacco, he was already showing signs of a slow bodily disintegration. Besides him, a number of so-called political suspects, men and women who had formerly had any connection with the Nazi party, were shipped off to another camp. It was late in the evening when they left, with only a short announcement just before they entered the train. This sudden impulse to move people on short notice during the night was a favorite Communist trick.

Thus our number became smaller and smaller. Now only one steam-shovel brigade and a wheelbarrow brigade remained. Our new brigadier, a twenty-year-old Pole by the name of Petrewitch, was introduced. I remember this day well because it was my father's birthday. We were then allowed to walk to our working place without a guard. In the beginning of this era a guard went along to see that we did not take our liberty too literally and try to escape. It was hard for us to understand that we were no longer under guard. In this short fall season we tried, during the short dinner break and after quitting time, to get as much extra food as possible.

The only trouble was, most of the field and forest fruits

113

had already been harvested during August by the Russians. But we still found some blueberries, mossberries, cranberries and stoneberries as well as a large variety of mushrooms and hips, which were precious tidbits for us. Besides that, we tried to glean from already harvested fields. All that, even though it was not too nourishing, helped to fill the stomach and kill our almost unbearable hunger drive.

PROPAGANDA EFFORTS

Only a few of the Reich Germans in our camp went along with the Communistic philosophy as it was presented to us. In general our ideas about the Soviets—their paradise and their system—was unanimous. We were too close to actuality and facts to be convinced in theory that anything good would result from this atheistic philosophy. Obviously a prisoner never has anything too good to say about the country which has forced him to work against his free will, but I think my statement is made without any bias.

Our political instruction was composed of lectures on current events with a Bolshevistic interpretation. One evening, for instance, we heard about the division of Germany into four parts. On another occasion we heard of the atrocities in the German concentration camps. When we heard for the first time how people had been burned alive, hanged, and their gold teeth collected, we were shocked. Although we had not been treated well, the German atrocities were too gruesome to be compared to our lot. These reports sounded unbelievable to many of us; other fellow Germans lost any of their remaining illusions about the righteousness of Nazi methods.

Time spent in the camp seemed like a small eternity to us. When I look back today, however, it seems as if the time—painful as it was—passed by very fast. How good it feels when memory reflects hard times in a somewhat milder sense and makes us forget.

114

10

CHANGE OF SEASONS

On May 10 the snow began to melt, allowing us to see something more of the things that surrounded the camp. Around us was a large field of stumps dotting the sandy soil. Here and there were a few cranberry bushes. The woods started about two miles away from the camp, beginning with a few scattered trees and developing into a dense virgin forest. The ground of the forest was covered with thick moss and sprinkled with blueberry bushes.

When the snow melted the roads became almost impassable. Knee-deep mud with deep ruts and puddles of water made traffic nearly impossible, since the Russians had not used gravel or hardly any rocks to improve the mucky dirt roads. We tried to walk on more elevated ground, for our cloth shoes with rubber soles were ill-fitted for that type of weather. On a dismal day in May, I walked home from the barn with another prisoner who had been in Russia before as a soldier. When a cart passed by with the horse waddling in the mud and the cart almost swimming on the

115

porridgelike puddles, my companion said, "You know what this reminds me of?"

"I have no idea."

"Well, one day during our spring offensive in 1942 in southern Russia we almost got stuck in the mud and pulled off the road to permit more energetic supply columns to pass. Suddenly we saw a German army cap floating on the flooded road. Looking closer I saw a face underneath. When I discovered that, I shouted at the soldier, 'Get up, you're drowning!'

"You know what he answered? 'I'm not here by myself. I'm riding a horse and leading a supply company.'"

It was a good story. How true it was in all its details, I did not know. But I did know that we endured a wet spring. The change from spring to summer did not last long. It was as if nature was in a hurry to make up for that which had been lost in wintertime. The sun climbed noticeably higher each day. The days were lengthened and the nights shortened. Around the time of summer solstice, instead of the night there were only two hours of twilight. One could feel that we were close to the northern polar circle.

With great anticipation all of us had been looking forward to the summer. We were tired of snow, of long, cold nights, and were eager to see the new grass and the flowers come out of the ground. We reminded each other about various plants and birds.

NEW TORMENT

But with the joys of summer came something else we had not counted on. All the other bad things concerning the Soviet paradise we had heard of had already happened to us; but this was something completely different.

Next in line as our worst tormentors—the Soviets taking precedence, of course—were the immense swarms of mosquitoes. With tremendous endurance they attacked us in wave after wave, trying to get the last drop of blood out of

116

our bodies. They preferred to bite our hands, feet and temples and, if given half a chance, they sucked themselves full with blood until they looked like little blood bubbles. Then they took off with a loud grumbling noise. These mosquitoes could make the quietest person nervous. Our only comfort was that they did not differentiate between the nationalities in choosing their victims. Guards were attacked with the same ferocity as we; the only difference was, they had more time to fight them. Our guard also had a mosquito veil; our only defense, even in the hot sun, was to wear gloves.

The summer did not last long. The vegetation period was only four months. During this time the plants sprouted, blossomed, and turned to seed. The duration of our work was not that short. The continual monotony of our labor dragged on and on.

As the summer season drew to a close, so did some of our privileges. The roving around in the time-off periods soon came to a close. The oncoming winter confined us once again to the camp. But then, in the evening we were exhausted anyway from walking all day in the snow and mud. The first heavy night frost came on September 14; the first snow fell as early as September 22. Thus, in four months, three seasons has passed by: spring, summer and fall. The worst was yet before us, the longest season—winter. The bleak meaning behind the word *winter* was significant; we had already experienced the Siberian kind. At the beginning of winter the snow melted a few times, but then it began to snow daily. Snowflakes fell without interruption. The sunlight lost its power to melt the snow as well as to warm and cheer us.

Toward the end of August the death rate had gone down. Several transports with sick people had been shipped to a hospital camp to die there. Most did not recuperate because their illnesses had progressed too far, and the trip to the hospital was particularly hard on them. The rest of the camp's inhabitants had become accommodated to the climate. Against the water mania we drank tea made out of brewed Scotch fir needles. Whether it helped, I don't know, but it didn't hurt anyone.

When the overseers saw that we were doing our work well, they then felt that they could easily make us work better. As an incentive we were permitted to write home. Each of us was given a postcard, and those who had exceeded the work norm got two. So on a rest day I sat down to write to my mother. I used the old address of our farm.

> DEAR MOTHER:
> This is the first time you are hearing from me. I am here in northern Russia. We are in a camp. You probably remember the pullover you gave me in case I should meet Father. I did not meet him. I have asked other people about him. Those who knew him at home did not meet him. There are lots of people here from our county, but none whom you would know. Mr. Kuhn from Gross Stoboi died on the way. So did Miss Hube. She always helped me.
> I am very hungry. In case you have more than we do, send me something to eat. Flour, peas, beans or anything you have that will not spoil. I would like to come home but I can't. Where are the others? Write as soon as you can. I'm homesick.
> Greetings to you all. Your loving son
>
> > HORST

Then I went to the guardhouse to mail my letter. After two or three weeks we looked anxiously for a reply. None of us got any.

CHAMBER ATTENDANT

At the end of September I came down with a fever for a few days. The doctor ordered me to become the chamber attendant of our barrack. With the help of two girls I had to scrub the floor. Besides that I had to see that we had water and wood and especially a warm house—which is essential

118

to living in Artic areas. Because of this job I soon felt better. However, this modification in my work did not last long.

Because of the frozen ground the ground-moving and steam-shovel jobs had ceased. When the dirt movers hit bedrock, it was extremely hard to make any progress without blasting the rock. But no blasting material was available. The camp administration, realizing that we might become unemployed or that the work done might not be profitable, decided to move us further north. This moving was not done all at once; the strongest men left first, accompanied by the equipment. The trip was not very pleasant for them since they had to ride on open platform cars. Our new camp was about 150 miles further north in the town of Malupera.

Hans left for a different assignment at this point. I had the privilege of remaining with the last fifteen men and then traveling by coach. We felt like gentlemen, particularly as we compared the way we had traveled before.

The coaches were furnished in a three-story fashion, with three wide benches having been placed on top of each other. Usually some slept on the upper ones, while others sat on the middle and lower benches. Wearing our prisoner clothing, we pushed ourselves into the overcrowded train, where there was only standing room. We set down the baggage beside us on the floor and then waited for the train to leave.

Finally the train got underway at about midnight. We had already traveled quite a distance when it stopped at a depot and a few Russians left the train. For some reason they were in a real hurry to get out of the coach. Since we prisoners were sitting or standing in the passage, they pushed us to the side. Suddenly we heard a cry: "My baggage is gone!" Obviously it had been taken along by several of the hurriedly leaving Russians. There was no time to start any search because the train was moving again and it was a complete impossibility anyway. But we prisoners had public opinion against us. We were reminded again that we were prisoners among free men.

Destination: Malupera

The train finally arrived at Malupera. We discovered we were not to be living in a regular prison confine but in three houses owned by the railroad which had been rented by the Third Column. The Russians had started to build a side track into the woods in order to get close to the virgin forest. Since this extension was not yet complete, the Third Column had taken over the job in order to build the railroad dam.

The following months rank as the worst experience in all my life. We had already endured some pretty bad times but they had not gone on so long. That winter at Malupera seemed endless in its severity. When we arrived the snow was already about three feet high and the ground was frozen quite deep; despite these conditions, we had to move dirt with wheelbarrows. Because I had lost so much weight, I could no longer do my former job.

I was finally put into the third category. Now my job was to level off the dirt dumped by prisoners pushing wheelbarrows, and then to clean off the wheelbarrows of any remaining dirt. Sometimes the dirt froze immediately after being thrown into the wheelbarrow, especially when it was dug up from deep in the ground and was still moist.

On November 6-8 the October Revolution was celebrated. The difference of date is accounted for by the old calendar used in Russia prior to the revolution. This meant relaxation for us; we were not required to work for three days.

Our barracks' walls were quite thin. In our room was a cannon oven which was supposed to keep it warm. But, no matter how large the fire, the warmth never lasted long. The oven had to be watched continually because, as soon as the fire went out, it became ice cold in the little room. This was especially tragic during the nighttime.

I was elected chamber attendant again since I had

gotten a good reputation for this job in the previous camp. The other prisoners thought my presence on this job would solve all related problems. They expected me to watch the fire day and night, and to get wood to burn somewhere in between. Because of the insufficient food and clothing and my poor health, this was a hard task. The woods were over nine hundred feet from the camp. The amount of snow increased daily until it was piled six to seven feet high. The railroad used a snowplow but we had to do our own shoveling. Wood-cutting was torturous because we needed almost a cubic yard each day. Because I could not saw very well alone, sometimes I went over to the girls' barracks and got their chamber attendant. However, if she helped me, I had to help her in return. Even during the nighttime I often had to go out to scare up wood. Frequently I got some from a pile on the other side of the railroad fill—wood which was supposed to be used later as building material.

On other occasions I borrowed the railroad repairmen's little pushcart which rode on one rail and had two wheels and was used to transport railroad ties. With that I went about half a mile away to a pile of firewood stacked up for the steam engines. From these piles I got several logs which were four or five feet long. But this method had its hazards; sometimes a train would come down the track where I was pushing the cart. When that happened I quickly had to throw both the cart and its contents to the side while the train passed. Naturally we were forbidden to get wood this way, but I did not know what else to do to keep our bodies from freezing.

Getting the wood there was only part of the problem. When I finally arrived with my load at the house, often I could not find anybody to help me saw the wood. From the little money we received I bought tobacco in order to pay my help, for this was a commodity that every prisoner would work for. Thus I had to spend my money for foolish wages, leaving less for myself. After the sawing, I split the wood. Sometimes in those low night temperatures I heard the bark of trees burst with a terrible crack.

Between the hauling and sawing of the wood I often went back to the barrack in order to look after the fire and warm myself a little. I worked until eleven or twelve o'clock at night in order to haul all the wood and to put it in a pile inside the door. Then I heated up the oven and lay down at about one o'clock. But as soon as I had fallen asleep, someone would pull on my leg and complain: "Attendant, the fire is out!"

I would rush out of bed, start a new fire again, and get it going—then lie down again. Before long someone was waking me again. It was an unbearable task. Although I tried to tell the men that they should feed the fire themselves, they felt that since I was responsible for it I could easily work during the night and sleep in the daytime. On the other hand, I could understand their anger, for they could not sleep when it was cold.

The barrack came awake at 6:15. After we had eaten something, at seven o'clock the brigade went to their work assignments, even though it still was pitch-dark. At about nine o'clock it started to dawn. I usually did a few chores in the morning and then lay down in order to get at least a little rest. But as soon as I did that, without fail a superior officer would come around and tell me that there was something wrong somewhere. Either the floor was not scrubbed or the beds were not in order or the toilet was overflowing.

DILEMMAS

Another plague in those days were the lice. In the former camp we had to take a bath at least once a week when our camp underwear was changed, but this camp afforded no such luxury. About every three or four weeks we were

122

taken to the public bath facilities. One day when it was very cold outside, the Russians ordered us all to go into the public bath; there we had to wash in the same room with the women. The Russians were never too strong on segregation of the sexes. In their atheistic philosophy all human decencies had vanished. To them man is only an animal and is treated with utter disregard to personal feelings.

During this time as a chamber attendant I had a run-in with a doctor. One of the men who was working outside did not have the kind of shoes needed in the far north. Leather shoes are too cold in the sub-zero weather, so the usual shoe is composed of cotton fiber having a rubber sole. The doctor told him to take mine since I didn't need them as a chamber attendant. I had to submit whether I wanted to or not. In the afternoon I needed some wood and, since I had no shoes, I had to walk on my quilted cotton stockings toward the woods and get some wood. I walked over there with the girl who was the woman chamber attendant. But the heels on my stockings were so worn that I was walking with my bare heels on the frozen snow. The next day I felt my feet burning. Discovering two large blisters, I went to see the doctor.

When I came into his office he did not hear me. He had his back turned toward me and was hugging the German woman who was our cook. I cleared my throat and they both jumped up. It was obvious from the doctor's face that he did not like the interruption. The cook left the room immediately.

"What do you want?" the doctor said gruffly.

"Oh, well—ah—I—" My words stuck in my throat.

"Come on, what's the matter with you?"

"Well, yesterday you told one of the men in our brigade to take my shoes because you didn't think I needed them. I had to go out and saw wood in the sub-zero weather and now my feet have blisters."

"Take your stockings off," he barked.

I did, showing him four silver-dollar-sized blisters, hoping that at least he would give me some ointment.

But as soon as he saw them, he said in German, for he had learned it in school: "You German pig, you did this on purpose to sabotage our socialistic effort. All you want is to go to the hospital and have an easy life!"

Had I not seen Russian hospitals from the inside? But what was the use. So I said, "Honestly, yesterday when—"

"Shut up! We'll fix you!" He lifted the phone receiver, dialed a number, and started to talk, pretending that he was talking with a superior officer and telling him about me and that they should come and get me.

Then he sat down and wrote a confession for me, saying that I had intentionally gotten the blisters. But I refused to sign the paper. That incensed him even more. He jumped up and yelled at me: "Get out of here, you lazy pig, this noon you will get nothing to eat!"

I put my stockings on and left his office. The cook was in the adjoining room. When I went past her she asked me why I made the doctor angry. I told her the story and also that I was not to get any dinner that noon.

"Don't worry," she said soothingly, "I'll see that you get food."

I wished I could have cried for Father or Mother. But nobody could have helped me in this situation. When noon came and all the others went to the kitchen, I had an unbearable feeling of hunger. But I saw the doctor was watching to make sure I did not get anything. So I waited till everybody had gotten his share and the doctor had disappeared in the adjoining barrack to eat. Then I slipped my empty can under my coat and took a detour to the kitchen. I peeked through the door and saw the cook sitting there eating. She beamed at me.

"Come right in," she said. "I saved a little for you."
She scraped the kettle into my can; I took it and left in a

hurry. From that day on the doctor always found fault with me and used every opportunity to give me a rough time.

CHRISTMAS

Thus we approached Christmas. The Russians, of course, did not appreciate this holiday. They were quite determined to work over the special days. But a miracle occurred which gave us more free days than we would have received at home for the annual celebration. At the first holiday on December 25 the thermometer went down to 50 below zero; and, according to the northern laws, we did not need to work outside when the thermometer was below 40 degrees. Except for the jobs that were necessary for self-preservation, all work was discontinued. The temperature stayed at this low point for four days.

Whether or not we really enjoyed those holidays is, of course, a different question. We had a little Christmas tree without candles in our room, but there was no Christmas spirit because everyone was engaged in his own self-centered interests. A few people told Christmas stories and talked about the good old days at home.

During this terrible cold wave it was impossible to work for a long time. Our ungloved hands stuck to the door handle; if we took our gloves off outside it did not take much longer than half a minute to freeze our fingers. The breath froze on our faces and on our work caps. We had all received nose binders to tie around our noses to prevent them from freezing. We had to watch our ears too lest they freeze, for it did not take long before they became white and stiff.

In those days around Christmas we often saw the phenomena of the northern lights. It was quite a performance with flashes bursting all over the sky in the colors of the rainbow. However, the northern people were never too impressed for the northern lights usually indicated a change of weather; and a change of weather there is usually for the worse—either a blizzard or more cold.

Meanwhile, most of us prisoners were completely run-down. I was five foot six inches tall and only weighed about ninety-eight pounds. Just moving about was hard enough, without trying to do any constructive jobs. But then came the saving news: the third category of manpower was to be shipped down to a hospital camp.

On January 10 there appeared a freight train with a prisoner coach hitched to it. This was a *stolypinsky wagon* named after a Czarist prime minister, Stolypin, and used for transporting prisoners. The prison car was already filled with Germans when we entered. Again it was a three-story car with a guard apartment in the front. An old sergeant was our guard for the trip.

South—we went south! This word had a magic sound for every prisoner who had been in the north. Thousands of hopes were attached to this word which could mean the difference between life and death, between innocent suffering or freedom. It was wonderful to go south.

The Ioccer Camp

Several days of traveling brought us to Ioccer. Right away we were put in the public bath. We were to shower while our clothing was being disinfected; this hygiene was absolutely necessary, for our clothing was inhabited by more than ourselves. Then we were put into the hospital.

Many familiar faces appeared in the camp hospital, among them Hans Rietger, my former friend from the Frische Haff. He was lying in the hospital because one of his legs had been frozen; it looked terrible. This young man had been one of the strongest and had always fulfilled his work norm. Now to see him lying there with his mutilated leg was pathetic. All his toes had been cut off and the wound looked quite bad; there was not much hope for healing since treatments were quite inadequate. He did not recover for a long time.

Our work group was reshuffled, and the largest percentage of our transport were put in the brigade connected with the hospital. The health of these men was supervised by a nurse who, in turn, was controlled by the camp doctor. In contrast to the northern circumstances, the food was rather good; the only trouble was that there was so little of it. Our diet included meat from animals such as horses, hogs and little pigs which had died for various reasons. The potatoes were partly frozen and already somewhat spoiled; but this bad food did not hurt us because we had become accustomed to dirt.

Our fellow sufferers here were the Moldauwanen, people who were a part of the Romanian countrymen. They had a bad reputation among us and the Russians for stealing everything they touched. They also showed a particular passion for trading but hated work.

Our daily work assignment was to get fuel from the woods three times a day. We had to carry it home on our backs, which wasn't terribly hard, and it even supplied needed exercise. Of course, with exercise our appetites increased too, but no additional food was provided.

In doing this job I became acquainted with a professor from Munich named Herbert Folger. While living with relatives in East Prussia, where he probably fled from the continual air raids in the western and southern German cities, he had been taken prisoner by the Russians in East Prussia. He had a Bible and a devotional book which he often loaned me, and for the first time I read the Word of God in the country of the godless. Admittedly, I did not necessarily read it because I felt like it, but rather because there was nothing else to read. This was actually the first time in my life that I had read large portions of the Bible.

I played chess with this man quite frequently. I had made the figures for the game and also had drawn up the checkerboard. While we were playing we often debated various problems. During one session I discovered he was quite an anti-Facist. Talking about the past was perhaps best, for no one talked much about the future; our horizon was limited and no one knew whether he would see his fatherland again. We had started to believe the Russian propaganda that Germany had been turned into a desert.

"Why all this?" I grumbled one day while playing chess with Folger.

"Well, in God's plan, everything has its order," he said. "Even the unpleasant."

"But I never killed a Russian," I insisted.

"Of course not, but most of us supported or went along with Hitler," he replied, moving one of the figures.

"But why are you here? You opposed Hitler, didn't you?"

"Yes, I did oppose Hitler, but not enough. Our nation has committed so many atrocities that somehow this had to be atoned for," he added.

"Do you really believe that the Nazis killed as many Jews as the Russians claim?" I asked, somewhat upset.

"Well, that I don't know," he replied. "But this much is sure: there were many persecuted and many killed and, in practically all the cases, for no good reason whatsoever."

"Do you think the Communists are better than the Nazis? They tried to steal your devotional book from you, didn't they, to use it for cigarette paper?"

He meditated a little and then looked at me with full assurance.

"Yes, they did all this; and, in the fullness of time their cup of iniquity will run over. I differentiate between the Russians as such and the Soviet leadership. Don't you remember that the simple, plain civilians nearly always had pity for us? Even the great Russian writer Dostoevski has written about people who showered political prisoners

128

with bread and other gifts. That is the reason they try to keep civilians away from us."

I did not know then who Dostoevski was, but I had to admit that what he said was true. For the Russian guards had always tried to keep civilians away from the train whenever it stopped on the way to our camp.

CHRISTIAN SERVICE

In the camp was a Protestant minister from Germany. He had been drafted into the army, and somehow had been caught by the Russians. Getting used to working by hand was hard for him because of his training and occupation. One day toward the end of the winter it was announced that he would conduct a service after the evening meal. A little stand served as a pulpit. After reading a text from a Bible, he expounded upon the portion. He said:

"Dear fellow prisoners, none of us is here in a situation to brag about. We have suffered tremendous hardships, many of us have died, and others have come close to death. Yet we know that according to the Scriptures, 'all things work together for good.' This will be hard to understand. But even the apostle Paul was afflicted with a certain disease. He had trouble in life too. But how about us? Can't we be compared to the Jews in the Old Testament? Weren't they led into captivity by the armies of Nebuchadnezzar?"

Why is he bringing that in? I thought. *Don't we need comfort? Now we are being compared to the Jews!* But he went on:

"And then they sat in Babylon. They had hung their harps on the willows and were weeping. We are weeping too. But perhaps more because we had to leave our home than for our sins, and they were great. As they forsook God, so did we. As they bowed down to idols, so

129

did we to Hitler. As they persecuted the prophets of God, so did some of us—or at least our leaders—persecute the church.

"But that is not all of it. Paul says: 'All things work together for good to them that love God.' In order to be reconciled to our situation we need to love God. And finally, there is a hope. God did not forget His people forever. Neither will He forget us. The Jews were finally permitted to leave the land of the captors. So will we. May God help us to this end. Amen."

Although I thought that praying for deliverance was a good thing, the idea of comparing Germans with Jews was not to my taste. I had not seen any persecution of the church nor had the papers reported it. I was upset by the sermon. So I went to Herbert Folger and complained: "I never heard about Hitler persecuting the church. I read the paper each day and I don't think that was ever reported."

"There are a lot of things you never heard of, young man," he replied. "But we have definite proof that the Nazis jailed priests and Protestant ministers. Some of them died in the Nazi camps."

"I don't think that's true," I countered. "And besides, didn't you hear about the priest who died when we arrived at the Ishma Camp?"

"That's beside the point. The Nazis committed unspeakable atrocities in the name of Germanic religion. Maybe the problem is not so much with the minister and what he said but with you! You are still too brainwashed in Nazi propaganda! You are hiding from the facts."

We argued back and forth and could not agree. I thought Folger was too stubborn.

Toward the end of February, Folger was made manager of the hospital's disinfection station. When the doctor told him that he could get himself a helper, he selected me. It was not easy for him to get along with the people for his thought life was different from that of the ordinary

130

camp inhabitants. It was also quite different from mine, but I at least tried to understand him. The job guaranteed an extra daily portion at the kitchen.

Sideline Job

The work was not too hard. The only unpleasant part was putting in and taking out the clothing from the hot oven, for the temperature was 220° to 236.° Our ears were constantly cracking from the temperature changes. This extreme heat was the only way to kill the lice and their eggs. We also had to collect wood and split it. But since we were not occupied full time, I was looking for some sideline job.

Meanwhile, we prisoners had become somewhat civilized, for each of us used a little board to carry his fish, bread and other food from the kitchen to his barrack. Since I did not have much to do, one day I drew some flowers on mine, took it over to the disinfecting station and heated a little fire hook in order to burn the lines out. When I had done this, the board looked rather attractive. When I took it back to the barrack I soon received orders for more decorated serving boards. In the beginning I decorated the boards for nothing, but when people began to offer me money for my work, I decided that I was not in a position to reject payment. I arrived at a fixed price of about three rubles per piece or its equivalent in bread or some other commodity. My customers were mostly the women and men of the camp, but I finally gained a reputation even among the Russian guards who ordered a few from me. The motifs which I selected were either specified by the order or according to my own imagination; there were landscapes from Germany or from Russia, flowers, branches, the four seasons, poetry, and many other things.

These sideline jobs became quite the fashion for us in northern Russia. The carpenters helped to make wooden suitcases, others were making cooking pots out of several tin cans, some were making brooms from birch tree branches and selling them to the civilians. Another sideline job was getting dry wood for the civilians who lived outside the fence, or doing other work for them in the evening. The women made new sweaters from old ones and sold them to each other or to the Russian women.

TRADING

Clothes trading received quite a boost. It had begun in the Ishma camp but here it was blooming. Through Russian or German intermediators the contact was made between the prospective sellers and buyers. These intermediators haggled over the price and, in so doing, received a share of the profits. Some of us sold clothing because a year ago we had received additional camp clothing. The Russians bought only things which were in good condition. They tried to lower the price as much as possible; their jobs were not the best paid ones either. Ability to pay usually depended on their income and position. In trade for clothing, we received tobacco, bread, cans, cereals or money. The reason for selling was always the same: most of us were hungry and needed bread. Some sold their heavier clothing in the expectation of the coming spring, since they thought they would not need them anymore.

As long as we had been watched by guards, such trade was prohibited. If the guard caught anybody taking shoes or something else out of the camp in order to trade with civilians outside, he usually confiscated the merchandise and paid the offender with a whipping. Nevertheless, during the long imprisonment many had found ways to get by and sell their belongings, thus saving themselves from starvation.

Without the guards the situation was more favorable. We even could go to the more distinguished Russians who

132

had more money, instead of being forced to trade with the poor laborers who worked with us. However, language barriers were obstacles for many of us. Thus, the mediators pushed themselves in between, knowing the language and the trade, but often keeping a large percent of the profit.

But this practice changed soon too; we all learned a little Russian and soon became as businesslike as the Russians themselves.

This so-called free market was openly tolerated by the government. Beside the railroad depot in all the larger cities and bigger towns was a market called a bazaar where everybody was allowed to buy and to sell whatever he wanted. A person could sell anything he had—even the clothes on his back—in the marketplace. Everything was sold and bought: shoes, pieces of bread, stolen potatoes, milk which had been produced above the state requirement, tobacco, apples and pancakes.

Prices were set according to supply and demand. An apple might cost ten or twelve rubles, a glass full of tobacco between five and fifteen rubles, according to quality. The buyer was allowed to taste the tobacco before he bought. Some of the strong smokers among us tried the tobacco of each stand till they had had enough, and then returned the next day or the next week to repeat their performance. Two pounds of bread at that time on the free market cost thirty to forty rubles—about fifteen to twenty dollars.

A JUST DOCTOR

The chief doctor at the hospital was a strict man but he tried to be just to everyone. The patients, nurses and all the others under his authority respected him. He was one of the few doctors who did not hate the Germans. We were accustomed to his own special method of diagnosis. If the patient had recovered so that he was able to work

133

outside again, he lined up before the doctor to be examined with the others who had recovered. Then the doctor looked sharply into each person's eyes. If someone could not stand his look, then the doctor asked in broken German: "Why don't you look at me?" He could not stand for anyone trying to hide a bad conscience. If someone was sick he could be sure that he would remain in the hospital as long as possible. And all of us were quite sure that most of his diagnosis had at least 99 percent certainty and really corresponded with the truth. When a patient was pronounced healthy, he was put in the working brigade again.

Because of his righteousness and his sympathies toward the Germans, the doctor was not too well liked among his Russian superiors. Occasionally he would intercede quite energetically before the camp administration for the sick in regard to food and medicine. Several high officers from Gnas Pogos came once to investigate the doctor's work. But since there was no evidence, they could not convict him and they left soon.

One prisoner had special luck with the doctor, but this happened accidentally. When his turn came to be examined, the doctor asked him, "What is your name?"

The man in question was an elderly man who had been a farmer from East Prussia. He answered, "Paul Gadomski!"

"What is your occupation?"

"*Bauer*" (farmer).

"Tomorrow to the kitchen."

This was the treatment the doctor prescribed for the elderly, grown-lean farmer. The secret of the story can only be realized by one who understands the Russian language. The doctor had understood the word *Bauer* which means *farmer* in German, but it means *cook* in Russian; thus the doctor wanted to do the supposed cook, who actually was a farmer, a favor and commanded him to go and work in the kitchen—always the most coveted job in a Russian prison camp.

11

TRANSFER

On May 24, 1946, I was transferred from the hospital to the twelfth working brigade of the Solchose. I was happy for the added weight and strength I had gained as a result of the extra pieces of bread I purchased with the income from my sidework. In the beginning we had to work in the woods, burning fallen trees and brush in order to make new pasture for the cows. Later we were moved to an outstation about five kilometers from the main camp. We were brought to the 145th Kilometer, so-called because of its distance from a large city along the railroad. This expression served as a substitute for a camp name. Our house was a new one which had just been built during winter. The resin was still dripping from the fresh wood from which it had been constructed.

We became completely independent from that day on. Everybody received his own bread, food and other ration cards, as well as some money for the work he did. It didn't amount to much, nor was it enough to buy all the things listed on our ration cards. Clothing was impossible to buy, for it was very expensive. We were very happy that at least we could buy what we wanted—as much as the ration cards allowed us—and did not have to be cheated in the mass kitchen. We also were allowed to cook our own food—one of the main joys of any prisoner.

This new brigade was composed of Moldauwanes, plus German women, girls, and men. We had a threefold mission: to quarry limestone, to saw wood, and to make hay. With crowbar, pick and shovel we walked over to the nearby stone quarry. Although it was only a small quarry, the work did not progress sufficiently to please the brigadier or the camp administration. There were too many small and too few big rocks. Even though the brigadier sat at the edge of the quarry and yelled continually, "*Krupni kamin*" (big rocks), it did not help much. We were picking and shoveling like mad, but the result was usually small rocks. The larger rocks were much more desirable for use in the two kilns which furnished our camp the necessary lime for whitewash, fertilizer, and sanitation purposes.

Two men built these kilns out of limestone. First they laid **a** foundation and then they built the arches for the fire holes. This had to be done with large rocks so that the smaller ones might be put in the middle. The furnace walls rose straight up, closing at the top like a pyramid. After the oven was smeared over with clay, it had to be heated by day and night shifts. Whole logs were pushed into the fire and burned. The fire was extremely hot. It took about twelve days and lots of sweat from the firemen to keep the fire going and convert the limestone to lime. The summer heat only increased the unpleasantness of that job for the two firemen.

BRIGADIER'S STORY

Our brigadier was one of those few Russians who appreciated anybody who did his duty well. It was his job to bring the work norm higher, but at least he also knew enough to pay tribute to those who had earned it and to appreciate their achievements. We wanted to work, for we knew that without work we would suffer worse hunger. Whoever was unable to work—be it Russian or German— could not make any money; this kept him from buying the food supplies which the ration cards allowed him; shortage of food, in turn, could bring death. The only possibility left for him would be to sell part of his ration cards at the black-market price in order to be able to buy the rest of his ration at the regular market price set by the government. With vegetables, nettles and other foods we tried to supplement our meals as much as possible. The work period was often long, and the thought of each man was the same: *How will I fill my stomach tonight? How can I make something extra?*

At the beginning the mosquitoes were not too bad. But when the limestone ovens were set up we had to go out and saw firewood for the ovens. Thousands of mosquitoes were sitting on every bush. The slightest movement of one of the branches chased up a cloud of them. Even the mosquito nets which we had received could not keep them completely away from our faces; besides that, our hands and feet were unprotected against the continual attack of the monster insects.

We had to saw wood for the furnaces. My sawing companion was a sixteen-year-old electrician's apprentice from Elbing by the name of Horst Schraemer who had been deported with his mother; he had been able to stay with his mother until their last assignment. Some of the days we were able to saw up to thirteen or fourteen cubic yards of wood, an achievement that surprised even our brigadier.

One summer day Horst and I did not know what time it was and thus came in a little bit early for dinner. When the brigadier discovered why we were there, he cursed us out till we told him that we had fulfilled our work norm for the day. He was quite surprised and could not believe that we had done so much in such a short period. After dinner he went with us to where we had been working and was surprised to see our big woodpiles. Sitting down on one of the piles, he called us to him. Then he shook hands with each of us and gave us a little reward. This was like a reconciliation on a lower level; anyway, it was an effort to show us some respect.

Watching him secretly, we observed that his face had assumed a strange expression. It was as if he actually had compassion for us. After he had meditated for quite a while, he broke the silence. At first his speech was restrained, but later he became more communicative and told us his life story in part.

He was a descendent of an ethnic Greek group that had settled in southern Russia. Before the war he had been drafted into the army and had been advancing toward sergeant. During the war his unit, stationed closed to Leningrad, had been encircled by the Germans. Since the unit expected imprisonment by the advancing German soldiers, they all threw their identification papers away. But the encirclement was not completed and the Russians were able to liberate this unit again. When the Red commissioners noticed that the soldiers had already considered themselves defeated, having made preparation to be taken prisoner by the German army, they told them to surrender their weapons and they were marched away. Thus they were taken out of the army and shipped to prison camps in northern Russia. That was how he had come to this Komi-Territory.

The Russians did not accept just anybody into their army as the Germans had done during the critical days of the war. On the contrary, many who were not of Russian descent were discharged. Those who belonged to another ethnic group were then shipped to Siberia or other prison colonies. Mostly involved in this measure were the Volga-Germans, the Greeks, and the Bulgarians. The Volga-

Germans still spoke the Swabian dialect as had their fore-fathers. They helped us as much as they could with our language problems, for they still knew German fairly well. As a rule it was not hard to make oneself understood in German in the north because the country was full of ethnic Germans who had suffered a fate similar to that of our brigadier. In fact, over a million ethnic Germans still live in Russia. This is only one of the minorities which make up more than 50 percent of the population.

Through our conversation we had come closer to the heart of this brigadier; after all, we all shared the same fate. And that was what unified us: the struggle for self-preservation in a hostile climate.

Harvesting in Siberia

After the limestone assignment was completed we were caught up with work in the hay harvest. This amounted to mowing the scarce swamp grass. Everybody received a scythe and started to work. But the problem was, very little grass grew on the swamps, making it hard to fulfill the work norm. Knee-deep we walked in the water while we mowed the grass, fighting the mosquitoes all the time. Often we became quite thirsty because a main part of our diet was salted fish which served as our meat substitute. Since no well was close to our barrack, we were forced to drink the water right from the swamp—the water loaded with millions of mosquito larvae. The Russians advised us to boil the water before using it, but no one could do that while working in the swamps which were a long way from home. Thus we often knelt down and drank the water even though it tasted terrible and did not really satisfy our thirst, but rather filled us with a good supply of mosquito larvae.

We also ate quite a few mossberries which remained from the previous year. Under the tremendous snow cover they had survived the winter and could still be eaten, in spite of the fact that the new harvest was in sight with green

139

berries already on the little bushes. On a free rest day I collected nearly a tin can full, selling them to the brigadier for eight rubles.

The advancing change of season was anticipated with mixed feelings. Even though fall brought a welcome enrichment of our menu, we all knew that the winter would follow right in its footsteps. Swamp after swamp was mowed. Meanwhile the new berries started to ripen in the woods. We used every free minute to pick them. Everybody ate until his mouth became sore. The two pounds of sugar which we received each month did not reach very far, especially since some of us sold part of our sugar on the free market in order to buy more bread and cereals which filled the stomach better. Especially during the berry time was there a rapid sugar trade. On the ration cards a pound of sugar cost five rubles but on the free market it brought sixty rubles. Among the Russians who lived outside the camp we always found customers.

At that time many of the Rumanians were discharged and were free to go home. Since their ration cards were valid only in the Komi-SSR, they had to buy a three- or four-week food supply for the whole trip. Sometimes they received as many as ten or fifteen loaves of bread besides their other food supplies; it was quite impossible for them to transport all that down to the south. Thus, they sold part of their bread, especially since they hoped the bread price would be lower in the Ukraine. They found out later that this assumption was wrong. The further south one went, the more expensive the bread became, for there had been a crop failure in the Ukraine.

It was quite amusing to learn about the crop failure. It had happened despite socialistic methods. Even the infallible Stalin was so fallible that he could not control the crops. In the spring of 1946 Stalin had proclaimed that we would be able to get along without ration cards by fall. We Germans were quite skeptical about the Russian promises.

Even many of the Russians did not believe the propaganda stories anymore.

The Russians had circulated among us a booklet which contained the story of Katyn, the famous place where about 10,000 Polish officers had been massacred by the Germans, according to their propaganda, after the war of 1939. The name of the German commander in charge of the execution squad and his adjutant were both specifically given. Especially interesting was the story of a Polish officer who was supposed to have escaped from the grave, a most spectacular thing! When these graves were discovered by the German army in 1941 the mass graves were inspected by an international commission and it was found that they originated from Russian executions. I, myself, and most of the other people in the camp read the book, not because of its content but only because we didn't have anything else to read. Silently we smiled over all the propaganda attempts. Had we not lived in a state which also had operated on a similar principle?

PARADOX OF FREE CHOICE

In the meantime the number of our brigade was continually reduced because of sickness. One day the brigadier told us we would be moving to another camp about eighteen kilometers on the other side of the Solchose. This news was terribly frightening for us, since we had heard from fellow prisoners that the circumstances there were almost catastrophical. But we could do nothing.

Our luggage was put on an oxcart and we sat on top. The move was made on a Sunday, a regular working day. Since we had to transport ourselves on a workday, this meant one day less of income. No one was in a particularly good mood. Our new brigadier, who had come with us from the old camp, stopped the column about noon,

141

indicating that we had reached our destination. Somewhat astonished, we looked around; we were somewhere in the woods. There was no camp, no shed, nothing that reminded us that humans had been there before.

"Make yourselves some barracks!" he told us. Soon after that pronouncement he left us there. Meanwhile he took another oxcart and went back for another transport of workers.

We were shocked. We did not have the necessary tools to make worthwhile building, and the nights were already becoming cooler. I was really boiling inside and so were others; I asked a few of them whether they would like to return to camp, but no one was really in favor of that. Only one person volunteered to turn back. With him and the driver of our oxcart, who was supposed to return anyway, I went back to our old camp the same day. No one especially welcomed us back, and during the night we had to sleep on emergency beds. The next morning we were brought before the *Naratchek,* a man who served as a type of labor representative in the camp. He also represented the camp administration and, as such, was not very enthusiastic about our return. He did not make much fuss over us but told us to return immediately. The only people who welcomed our reappearance were those who also were dissatisfied with the methods the Reds used.

Since we had a little bit of baggage we could not walk again to the other camp. We were supposed to go there the next day on a truck, but the next day was a holiday and no truck went. Another day came and again there was no truck. In the meantime we were pushed into the third brigade so that we would be occupied during the delay. After a while we were forgotten. I have never regretted taking that step. Although I was not very calm on the inside, I still felt that my disobedience was justified. On the other hand, the disobedience was a risk by which I put to a test the possibility of free choice in a state administered by the Communistic system. What we had been saved from became obvious when the other workers from the new camp returned after a few months. Looking like skeletons, they were sick and dirty, with torn clothes. Some were put into the hospital, but others died.

At that time I hated anything Communistic, anything Russian. I was ready to take revenge whenever I would have a chance. I was so fed up with the whole system that I could not change the unforgiving attitude I had acquired. I had never known God's standard of forgiveness: as often as seventy times seven. I had never thought that He would expect me to meet His requirements to be tolerant and kind to the other person. As mentioned before, I had no experience of the forgiveness in Christ for myself.

REVENGE

I had to ask myself: Were not the Russians people the same as we? It was obvious that they had been taken in by false propaganda. And of course the taste for revenge comes naturally; in fact, they did just what we had done with them while we were victorious. In all fairness, I had to admit that we were no worse off than their own prisoners. On the contrary, we often had better jobs than some of their own political prisoners.

The bitter spirit of those days has passed away since I have experienced God's love for myself. My position today is that I forgive all men, even a Russian, even a Communist. If I cannot love my fellowmen, then I am certainly not deserving of the love of God.

During the summer of 1946 I became the driver of a team of oxen, a responsibility which brought in a little more income. Even though the oxen were the worst animals around the camp, they were still capable animals. But I was often angry with them. They were supposed to be directed with the help of a stick. When I hit the left ox on the left side of his back he was supposed to turn right, and vice versa. I did everything wrong at the beginning, but finally, after I had degenerated to the black sheep in the brigade, I caught on to the tricks of the other drivers.

Even then I could never reach the work norm, not only because the oxen were terribly lazy and hungry, but also because I was too particular with my work. I had suffered from undernourishment for about eighteen months, and as a result I had a hard time keeping my thoughts concentrated on what I was doing. Often I forgot to bring the wagon home from the field. This absentmindedness developed to the extent that I couldn't even get along with myself, a condition which contributed to my spiritual degeneration.

One of my main jobs was to haul wood. But I did not know the local circumstances and was not familiar with the roads and the places where I could find the wood. Sometimes when I managed to find a pile of wood and got it loaded, the oxen would break into a cabbage field and turn the wagon upside down. So I would have to reload the whole load. Many accidents happened to undermine my waning self-confidence.

Our norm was 2.1 cubic yards per day, which meant that we had to haul three wagons with 0.7 cubic yards at a time, for it was impossible to make more than three trips a day. According to Western measurements this might not be much, but for Russia it was quite a bit since both the oxen and the wagon were small.

When we came to the lumber yard, the amount of our load was guessed by an official guesser. The older drivers knew this man pretty well and probably once in awhile gave him something so he would make a good guess on their loads. Since I had nothing to give him, my load never came into a higher bracket whether it was really full or not. One day I got excited about his unfair guesses and spoke to a superior, but this made the situation even worse.

I was so discouraged that I finally decided honest work was impossible under these conditions. From that day on when I was traveling over the countryside I watched for any available woodpile and a road leading to it. I knew that many of these were intended for other purposes, but I tried to suppress my conscience because no one else was conscientious about it except the superiors. The only hazard I had to be careful about was that none of the officials saw me loading. But once the wood was loaded, no one was concerned about where it came from.

One day I had what seemed to be especially good luck. The road to the woods in which I was supposed to load led over a log bridge which had recently been almost destroyed when a caterpillar tractor crossed it. Looking around and seeing no one in sight, I loaded the planks on my wagon and drove away as quickly as possible. It was easy that day to fulfill the norm. The next day two people were sent to repair the bridge. But they had to return home because there was no bridge to repair. I had taken it to the woodpile.

At first sight, the norm system looks very practical. Someone who does the work of two also receives the wage of two. But this often is determined by the favor one has with his superior. On the other hand, someone who is weak or sickly gets paid for only as much as he can do. A low income means less to spend for food, and less food hinders any development toward improving the situation.

DEHUMANIZATION

The continuous competition made the men into robots. Hatred and mistrust toward our neighbors were noticeable everywhere. The evilness within man which usually does not appear so much in normal times seemed to reign in that country.

145

There is a common misconception about the zeal of the Communists. It is reported that they sacrifice everything to reach their goal, which is world revolution. This is true wherever Communists are in the minority, fighting for their existence and for more power; but this zeal dies away as soon as they are in the majority and have gained control of the government. This is the same phenomenon that occurs in any group when it settles down and starts to divide up the spoils gained as the fruit of suffering. Communists are just as selfish as any other unregenerate people.

Communists like to talk of their doctrine of equality, but I am convinced that equality exists no longer than for one day after the Communist government has been created. The next day it needs civil officers, army officers, and a hierarchy in order to administer the affairs of the country. These jobs are held, of course, by only a select group; they are chosen because of their intelligence, cunning, or because of their brutality or other influence. In order to work on a higher level, one of course expects higher wages. The general receives much more income than the ordinary soldier, and also the farm administrator receives more money than the laborer. Is that equality?

None of these elite would want to have his sons start out the same way their father did. So the children are put in better schools and are always promoted more quickly; for example, one of the children of Stalin very soon became a general in the air force, although not having a superior intellect.

POTATO HARVEST

Life in the prison camp was adjusted to the seasons. Now the end of the summer had come, and with it new problems. On August 30, 1946, the potato harvest started at the *Solkhoz*. They could not wait any longer since the

146

frost was already beginning. This was an important development for us.

In order to demonstrate that we had new freedom, the Russians had earlier torn down the fence which had been around the camp. Thus we could walk out on each side of the camp without being checked. Although there were some guards at each field, everybody took as much extra food as he could carry into the camp. There were potatoes, turnips, and cabbage which we cooked in large quantities and ate with great relish. Now at last we could really fill our stomachs. Even though the vegetables had no fat and no meat, the main thing was that we could eat our fill, thus easing that constant gnawing of hunger.

The method we used to harvest the potatoes was very primitive. Each person received a three-pronged fork with which he dug the potatoes and put them into boxes. A Volga-German counted and kept records of the boxes. The pay was figured upon the number of boxes we had filled. The drivers had to load the boxes on trailers and bring them to the storage room. Usually three or four of these wagons had to drive together and were guarded by a former nurse, whose job was to watch that none of the potatoes were sold to the civilians along the way. In the storage room the potatoes were received by the deputy brigadier and the boxes counted again.

The potato plants were hauled to silos in order to be stored and fed to the cows during the wintertime. However, the filling of the silos began when the frost had already turned the leaves black. Thus it did not make very good silage.

Later, after the potatoes were sorted, they were hauled to the railroad depot which was about one mile away from the farm. The depot included a storage room and an office for the guard. The potatoes were dumped into the storage room and then shipped away from time to time. For this procedure there usually was a representative of the farm as well as a representative of the other enterprise which was to receive the potatoes. Everyone watched that none of the helpers stepped on the scale while the potatoes were weighed.

Every shipment in Russia, especially if it was foodstuffs, was escorted by the representative of the party who was supposed to receive the load. He had to watch along the way that none of the goods disappeared. If this precaution had not been taken, many boxcars would have arrived empty at their destination.

Toward the beginning of September we learned that a new transport of female Russian and Polish prisoners was supposed to be put in the empty camp barracks. We wondered how this could be, since the fence which had surrounded the camp at our first arrival had been torn down the past spring. We were soon made aware of the next step. The whole job of putting up a new sixteen-foot fence was to be done all over again.

As soon as the new batch of prisoners arrived, camp discipline became severe once again. The female prisoners were mostly collaborators who had cooperated with the Germans. Most had been sentenced to between ten and fifteen years of forced labor. One woman had been condemned to five years of forced labor because she had stolen two pounds of cereal. Others had served as nurses in the German army or as secretaries in the German antiaircraft division at home.

Since the Rumanians had left during the summer, the Germans had occupied most of the better jobs in the camp. While the Russian prisoners always had to line up at the gate in brigades to be counted, we Germans could walk in and out as we pleased.

HOMESICK AND HUNGRY

Life was much easier now than it had been in the beginning of our capture, but most of us were bothered with a terrible homesickness which was a burden on our souls as heavy as that of a physical ailment.

At home the apples were ripening on the trees and the children were running around barefooted; the season was the opposite in Russia. Blizzards raced over the country and rattled doors and windows, and there were five to six feet of snow. Hardly any of us had enough clothing to keep our bodies warm.

At home our mothers (or the wives of the older prisoners) would have patched the stockings and repaired the other clothing. But here we were occupied with farm jobs all day; in the evening we had to cook, and then everybody was so tired that he only longed for bed. The rest days were all occupied with doing other chores which had piled up during the week. We often turned the last ruble around in our hands and asked ourselves: *Are you going to buy a piece of bread for your stomach or some clothes to cover your body?* It was a difficult choice to make.

At home even at the end of the war we could sit down to a full table, but here things were different. Our constant hunger is hard to describe; however, this much can be said: it was a very unpleasant feeling, and it led to a complete breakdown of character. None among us desired more physical activity than was absolutely necessary. No one thought of sports. Although there were more German women than men in the camp, there was no courtship until toward the very end of camp life. Most of the men dressed sloppily, and shaving was a luxury engaged in only over weekends. Sarcasm and hostility substituted for humor and courtesy. All higher idealism had vanished because of the terrible hunger drive—a drive which becomes a god and controls the man who doesn't have enough to eat.

Often as I saw the others march to the kitchen when I didn't have any money to buy my coupons; when I had to

149

see how they prepared their own meals and sat over the porridge like hungry wolves; when I saw others in superior jobs bringing in extra food in the evening, I would pull my blanket over my head so I couldn't see what was going on. My longing for food was bad enough without making it worse by watching others eat what I did not have and could not afford. And in the evening when I looked into the clear sky with its stars, I thought nostalgically that the same stars were shining at home.

My eyes became wet; I was only a youth, just seventeen years of age. I couldn't help but wonder why this was happening to me. And sometimes I recalled the words of a song we had learned in catechism instruction meetings at my home church:

> "Aus Tiefster Not schrei ich zu Dir"
> Out of the depths have I cried unto thee, O LORD.
> LORD, hear my voice:
> Let thine ears be attentive to the voice of my supplications.
> If thou, LORD, shouldest mark iniquities, O LORD,
> Who shall stand?
> But there is forgiveness with thee,
> > that thou mayest be feared.
>
> PSALM 130:1-4

But, as far as reaching out to God, I didn't know how nor did I try. It was enough for me to realize there probably was a God—but that He could help me or liberate me from my troubles, I did not suspect.

FRIENDSHIP

One noon I was able to finish my work a little earlier than usual. I unhitched my oxen and took them to the barn. After feeding them some hay, I left the barn to get my own dinner. On the way to the camp I met Günther, one of our drivers, whose oxen were trudging slowly through the deep snow. Günther, a lad of seventeen, was standing on the sledge, his fur cap covered with frozen breath. He looked depressed.

I attempted to cheer him up. "No wonder the oxen aren't in much of a working mood—the way you look."

"I'm not in a mood to joke, Horst."

"Well, excuse me for hurting your feelings!"

He stopped his oxen and looked into my face as if he wanted to tell me something, provided I would get him started.

"What's the matter with you? Was the brigadier too hard on you?"

"No, it's not that." He added, "Today I did something that will haunt me the rest of my life."

"What happened?"

Günther looked around to make sure no one was watching us or listening.

"You remember that the brigadier told me to drive to the camp and await further orders at Barracks No. 5?"

I did not exactly remember that, but after the brigadier had talked to him, I had seen Günther proceed in the direction of that barracks. Germans did not live in them. They were occupied by the Polish and Russian women that the guards had recently brought to the camp.

"Well," he continued, "I went there, thinking I might have to help move some bunks or the water barrel. But when I went in, one of the women guards met me and asked me to pick up the body of the women who had died that night. And when I saw the first one, I somehow had the feeling that I was looking into my mother's face. It was too much for me; I could not bear to lift her. The woman guard barked to a few others who had been permitted to stay inside the barracks on account of sickness and they lifted her body onto the sledge."

"But it wasn't your mother," I told him.

"No, I know that, but I had often talked to this Polish lady. She had worked for us on our farm in East Prussia and we had always gotten along real well. A few weeks ago she gave me some bread and, as you know, when a Slave gives you bread, this is a sign of friendship. She even mended my stockings. Occasionally I brought her some firewood because she was often so cold; she couldn't stand this climate and the poorly heated barracks." He sighed. "You know," Günther added in a more reverent voice, "I think she was a believer. What she did to me she did unto Christ. Now she is gone."

I tried to comfort him. But he had so much on his mind that I let him talk.

"They put two more dead bodies on the sledge. And then the guard gave me a description of the graveyard, which was about two miles away from camp. She said they had already dug the graves. But it had snowed and I had to go through high snowdrifts. The three corpses often fell off the sledge; and since their eyelids had not been closed, they always seemed to be looking at me. I hardly had the strength to put them on the sledge again. It was almost as if they didn't want to be buried there."

"What did you do then?" I asked.

"After I got to the graveyard, I saw sticks with numbers on them sticking out here and there in the snowdrifts—many of them. But I couldn't find the newly dug graves; the snow had already covered them."

I looked at the sledge. Since the corpses were not on it, I asked the obvious question: "Where did you put them?"

"That's just it," Günther muttered, tears dripping from his eyes. "I hit another snowbank in the graveyard and the bodies fell off; I just didn't have the strength to put them back on again."

He was so overcome by emotion that he could hardly speak anymore. The oxen, who had waited while he told me all this, were becoming restless.

"I think you're too weak now," I said. "Let me take care of the oxen. You go and eat something, or you soon—" I could not continue. "Perhaps when the snow melts, we can go there and bury them," I finally added.

"Not a bad idea." Günther turned around and stumbled through the snow while I took care of the oxen.

12

COMMUNISTIC MORALS

Since our prison camp life was so monotonous, people tried by various means to escape from its boredom. One way was to follow the lead that Communistic Russia promoted—the idea of free love. Many people carried out this permissive practice. It was not even shocking to most of the Russians because when the church and Christianity were outlawed, ethics went too. The teachings of evolution were advocated by the Russians, with the inevitable conclusion that man was regarded as merely a higher type of animal. Espousal of this belief allowed free expression of any animal drive, satisfaction of the sexual instinct being one of them.

We had already come in contact with this practice of free love during the occupation, and it was carried on in all the different concentration camps. One of the most common practices was for women prisoners to sell themselves to their superiors in order to receive better pay or higher ration cards. Men and women usually slept in separate barracks with as many as thirty people in each, but it was not unusual to see a man and woman making love while other prisoners were in the same room. A sense of shame was almost unheard of in that godless society. Free love was also practiced by some of the German men when their material circumstances improved. This was especially true of those who had better-paid jobs and received higher rations. Whether married or unmarried, they used their extra pay for such indulgence.

As an illustration of how low the morals had sunk, there was an unmarried Russian teacher in the camp who had four illegitimate children by four different men, and a fifth one was on the way. This was supposed to be an "example" for the nation. Stalin gave another example by divorcing his wife and being married to three others in succession. The Russians refer to the marriage ceremony as being "written together" and to the divorce act as being "written apart." Often the people didn't want to get married because there was a small specified fee for the first divorce, an expense which increased with the second and third divorces.

The Russian government used to encourage the birth of illegitimate children. After their arrival, the children were gladly received into the state-owned kindergartens. Here from infancy they were given superior food and special training. This early independence from home very soon develops self-confidence in the child and less dependence upon his parents than otherwise possible. Thus a person was created who was well fitted to propagate the devilish theories of Marxism.

Often mothers sold themselves to the men in order to provide food for their children. This solution did not help the situation much, for soon more offspring were expected. But in general the buying of women was a very common practice. This was especially possible in a society where there were many basic needs and the people would do anything for food to eat; girls sold their virginity for a pound of bread. Several of our women were pregnant when they returned to Germany.

154

Although I did not learn of any case of venereal disease within our camp, it is possible that such things were kept under cover. I was told later by my mother that this happened quite frequently at home. In our village, from which almost everybody who was able to work had been taken away, the Russians had left a few younger women who had little children. Four of them, I was told, were infected by this disease and died during the time of occupation because there was no available medicine to cure them.

The promise of women was often used as an encouragement for the exhausted soldiers of the Red Army to try their best in a proposed attack. Earlier in the war the officers had used vodka to intoxicate the soldiers so that they would run into the German machine guns. This tactic caused very high losses without much gain. But with this new method the soldiers had clearer minds and knew better what they were doing. Thus they were more effective during the attack, and the promise which had been made to them kept them going. Attainment of food, drink, and the use of a woman was the highest goal any member of the Communist society could covet—at almost any level.

In the prison camps a whole new system of marriage morals came into practice. An officer in our camp had left his wife and four children in the Ukraine. During his imprisonment he finally managed to come into a superior position. While there he established himself in a common-law marriage with a girl who bore him several children. When his term was up he said good-bye to his northern lady and family and left for the south to rejoin his first wife.

NEW APPOINTMENT

Many of our fellow comrades had been moved to distant camps where their situation was sometimes worse, sometimes better. One of my friends, a former cowhand from East Prussia, was working in the barn brigade. He was about forty, heavyset in appearance, and one who knew his way around. He had children himself at home but of course he

155

did not know where they were now. Feeling drawn to him as a substitute father, I spent some time with him, and we often talked about bettering our situation.

One evening he came into the barracks. It was after supper but most of us had not eaten enough. He brought a can of porridge along which he had gotten from the hog kitchen where he was working. I smelled the food.

"You are well off," I said to him as he passed by.

"What makes you think so?" he asked.

"At least you have something besides your ration," I replied.

"You want something?"

I had little reason to say no. So I said yes, got my can, and received a helping. While we sat eating, I casually asked him if there was an opening for me where he worked.

"Why, do you want to change jobs?" He grinned.

"Of course I do. I have been hungry every day since the winter started. For a change I would like to have a full stomach like I have tonight."

"Can you drive oxen?" he asked after some thought.

"I tried but it did not go so well; I understand yours are better fed. I think that would make it easier."

"Well, I will mention this to my brigadier. He is a Volga-German and I think you would like working with him."

With this exchange we parted. The next day I had the job. He was right; the brigadier accepted me right away. I realized my good fortune—or was it destiny? This was one of the most coveted jobs.

As far as eating was concerned, we received special privileges on this job. We received three extra meals besides our ration card. My work consisted of hauling firewood, hay and straw, silage and sawdust. There was so much to do that often I did not know what to do first. Routine soon set in. Because we worked with animals, we observed no Sunday or holiday. Our hours were until about seven o'clock at night, which was quite late since the night up there starts

156

in the wintertime between 2:30 and 3:30 in the afternoon. This is especially noticeable because the temperature drops immediately when the sun goes down.

In the morning we began at seven o'clock. My job started with the cleaning, feeding and watering of the animals. The watering was a special problem since we first had to break a layer of two-inch-thick ice on the water containers. Then we started to clean the stable, which was a difficult task in wintertime because the manure had frozen to the ground. After that was done we started our regular working routine.

BUTCHERING

The special days there were the butchering days. The Volga-German brigadier and a butcher from East Prussia by the name of Franz Gottschalk did the butchering. The slaughterhouse was a wooden barrack separate from the others. Usually the animals were killed by the brigadier. For this he used a dagger which he ran into the neck of the animal, paralyzing it completely. Then he cut the throat open. Once I watched him when he had to butcher a goat. He just grabbed it by its horns and cut the throat open so that the blood sprayed around the room. I thought it was quite cruel although all of us by now were accustomed to all kinds of cruelty.

The entrails were thrown out into the snow. Soon all kinds of hungry people gathered there in order to scoop them up. Cleaned and cooked, the entrails made a meal. When hogs were butchered they were usually skinned. The butchers trimmed off the skin in such a fashion that much fat remained on it. As soon as the meat had been delivered, and the skins had been hung up, they peeled off the fat and kept it for themselves.

They had a rule that there always had to be an officer of the *Solchose* present at butchering day. Meat, especially pork, was the best black-market merchandise. For the regu-

157

lar ration cards the people usually got only horse meat or dead pigs. Toward the evening, when everything was done, we drivers had to haul the meat to the *captiorka* or storage room.

Arriving with my sled, I was just in time to see something falling into the snow. The meat inspector soon appeared. He looked the butcher, a German prisoner, straight into the face. "Is everything here?" he asked.

"Yes, sir," the butcher replied without blushing.

But the inspector did not believe him. He counted the individual pieces such as the hearts, legs and tails. There was usually none of those missing. Then the meat was weighed.

We loaded the meat on the sledge and off we went, the inspector guarding the convoy closely. We knew well enough that there was no chance of helping ourselves at this point.

After we had unloaded everything except the hides in the *captiorka*, the meat inspector left. All that was left for us to do was to hang the hides over a crossbeam in the barn. When we had done that, I saw our brigadier take out a knife.

"What are you going to do now? Do you want to butcher a hide?" I joked.

"Just wait and see." He grinned. And now he carefully cut off several pounds of meat he had left in the hide on purpose.

He gave me some of it but said, "But will you keep your mouth shut?"

"Of course, I will," I assured him.

"OK then, let's go and get the utensils," said the German butcher.

"I thought you had everything."

"No, I've got to go back once more. You want to go along?"

"I will if you insist," I said, "but let me first bring the oxen into the barn."

I unhitched the oxen, brought them into the barn and gave them hay and water, then we went to the slaughterhouse.

Just as we came around the north end we saw a shadow.

The butcher stooped down and said a bit overly loud, "Did my knife drop here?"

"Well, I did not see it," I replied.

At this the shadow dashed around the corner. It was the meat inspector. He regarded us suspiciously and looked especially at the butcher, saying, "What are you doing here?"

"I lost my knife, and besides, I wanted to cut a little fat off the entrails!" the butcher replied with a quick presence of mind.

At this he pulled the knife out of the snow and started working at the frozen entrails.

The meat inspector probed the pockets of the butcher's jacket, but finding no meat, he said, "OK, take what you want, but next time you'd better be careful. I don't like to see you around here after working hours." Satisfied, he left us alone.

The butcher waited until he was sure the inspector had disappeared; then he started to search the area where I had seen something fall into the snow earlier, and finally he lifted about four pounds of fat meat from the ground.

"How do you like that!" he said.

"Not too bad; it takes us at least half a year to get that much in rations," I replied.

"Well, here take some; you young fellows need a little extra. Too many have died already."

"You are very thoughtful," I answered, "but isn't it stolen?"

"Did you not tell me that the Russians took all your cattle when they came to your home?" he asked.

"Yes, that's true; they took our livestock," I admitted.

"How many were there?"

I answered his question after mentally calculating. "We had about twenty-five milk cows and at least that many heifers."

"All right, Horst. Who did the stealing?"

The answer was obvious and I realized how foolish it was to hesitate. I took the meat he sliced off, hid it in my pants legs and gloves, and left the scene. I walked away with a stiff gait, handicapped by the food I was concealing.

Before long we approached the guardhouse.

"I hope they don't search us today," I remarked. My friend agreed.

I let him go first and he was not too pleased with that. The guard let him go through but stopped me. I wondered if the meat inspector had told him to search us.

"What have you got there between your gloves?" he barked, grabbing at them. Out fell the meat, about three-quarters of a pound. Then he pounded me and made me take off my coat. When he couldn't find anything more, he kicked me in the back and said, "*Pasholl!*" or "Get out of here!" I cleared out as fast as I could but I could still hear him cursing behind me.

I soon reached the barracks where I found that the butcher was already frying some meat. He grinned at me. "Did they search you?"

"They sure did," I said in a depressed tone.

"Good thing I only gave you a small piece," he consoled.

"Well, they didn't find everything," I said as I pulled a half-pound piece of meat from my trousers.

"Good job." He smiled. Then he sliced a piece of the fried meat and gave it to me.

"Remember," he cautioned, "you've got to survive. Those of us who have made it this far must get out alive to tell the others what the Russians did to us here."

FATE

The butcher was a rare comrade. Other men I met were not this unselfish. But my circumstances were improved for other reasons.

The new brigadier, Kossa, was a bear of a fellow—strong, husky, and unusually friendly. The first few days I had trouble adjusting to the new job but I tried to work as well as I could. It was important that I keep this job; otherwise I didn't know how I could make it through the winter.

When I lost some hay, Kossa helped me reload it. He also showed me where to get a little extra food. This was actually a type of porridge which was cooked for the pigs. Standing in the hog kitchen one day, I asked him how he had gotten to the camp himself.

"Oh," he said, "don't remind me." His usually friendly face became clouded and I could see that he was deep in thought. Thinking that I had probably struck a particular source of heartache, I told him out of pity that we didn't have to talk about it.

"That's not the trouble," he murmured in a depressed tone. "You are a German citizen, and you might be sent home someday, and there you can tell what happened here."

"Are you kidding?" I said. "Do you really think that they will ever send us home?"

"Well," he replied, "I have heard from other camps that they sent German prisoners home."

"I hope you're right, but what does that have to do with your fate?" I asked.

"Well, this much. You're a German citizen, and it might be said that you're being required to suffer for the deeds of the SS and the German army even though you yourself may have been innocent. But we—we who are Russian citizens—have ancestors who came here before 1800. Our cultural heritage was handed down in the German language; this background has become our crime."

I still couldn't understand that what he was relating had anything to do with the reason he was working here.

"It all happened when Hitler attacked Russia," he continued. "Stalin was afraid we Volga-Germans would rise up and join hands with fellow Germans—an event which we had not planned—and so the police gathered us up and shipped us here to the polar circle, and our women were sent someplace else." Kossa sighed. "And now we are here."

"Did they give you a hard time?"

161

"Worse than that. We were stationed at a camp close to the Petchorra River and forced to build a bridge over it."

"Did they give you just as little to eat as they give us?"

"Well, Horst, believe me, our food rations were much worse than yours now. Between six hundred and eight hundred grams of bread is your portion. Do you know how much they fed us?"

"I have no idea."

"Listen to this. We were given only four hundred grams a day and there was absolutely no way to get anything extra."

"Did many die?"

Kossa had become excited as he related what had happened. But when I asked that question, he became very melancholy again. "One morning I was sleeping under my dirty blanket," he said. "Around 6:30 the guard came and shouted at us that we should get up. So I got up. But I noticed that my neighbors did not rise. So I knelt down and shook the one to my right, only to find that he had died. Then I turned to the one to my left, and discovered the same fate. He did not stir; he had been overcome by death during the night.

"That's not all," he added, seemingly lost in thought. "After breakfast we went to the bridge which was being built high over the river about two hundred feet in the air. Two of my buddies were carrying stops. One was so exhausted that he stumbled and fell off the bridge into the water, taking his colleague along."

Kossa could usually control his emotions. Most of the time he was a jolly fellow. But now I saw that his eyes were getting wet.

The milking in the barn was done by several trustworthy Russian women of the *Solchose*. The women had quite a work advantage over the caretaker in the barn, who had to be present to receive the dung with the shovel as soon as a cow lifted its tail. Woe to him if he fell asleep during his twelve-hour shift and a cow lay down in the dung! She had to be washed right away. As a rule the animals were treated very well and, in contrast to the prisoners, received as much to eat as they wanted. I often talked about this paradox with a girl who was in charge of the calves' nursery. She slept there and was required to render twenty-four-hour service to the calves.

PROSPERITY

The dream of every prisoner—besides getting his freedom back—was to get a well-paid job. All of life circled around eating. Everybody was willing to work as much as he could if he could only fill his belly. When a person finally had managed to get a good job, he usually sold a part of his ration cards and started to save. Everybody tried to use a profitable time as wisely as possible in order to have some reserve in case of an unexpected setback, which happened frequently and without any previous warning. The most coveted jobs were those of the carpenter, smith, driver or watchman.

Among my fellow Germans, comradeship was on a steady decline. Everybody was a neighbor only to himself; but, in spite of that, it never came to the place that one allowed his fellow prisoner to suffer starvation. Nevertheless, the mostly sub-zero weather, the rough life of a prisoner, and the work-norm drive caused the hostility among us which the Russians had intended. Resentment between us could not be completely avoided.

My friend, Kaufmann, the baker from Elbing who had told me about American prison-camp conditions, had been hospitalized. In the spring he was pronounced well enough to work regularly. He pitched in for awhile, but he always had trouble with his one leg because it was shorter than the other. In his spare time he had been asked by the baker to help out in the bakery. We all envied him because we knew that at least he could eat enough.

Later on he complained to the doctor that he could not

work in the fields and he was assigned full time to the bakery. Usually in the evening he sold his ration bread or some extra bread he had brought home. Many of the prisoners, Volga-Germans or Russians, were his customers. One day in particular I overheard him bargaining.

"How much do you want?" asked his customer, a tall, blond Volga-German named Fritz.

"Thirty rubels a kilo," said Kaufmann.

"That's way too much."

"If you can find anything cheaper, go ahead and buy it."

Fritz did not like the flippant answer. His face was marked by the many hardships he had experienced. The process of growing up in the USSR had made him tough. Now his usually placid expression changed to a tense, demanding one.

"I can get bread for twenty rubels and even for nothing." Fritz kept on trying to bargain Kaufmann down. But we all knew where he had gotten bread for nothing. He had simply stolen it. Since he was always surrounded by a gang of tough boys, nobody ventured to get things back from him. Now he looked Kaufmann straight in the face and threatened him: "You'd better sell me a kilo or else you might be sorry for it!"

Kaufmann knew that he was cornered and couldn't push Fritz any further. He was obviously intimidated by the gang of fellows with Fritz.

"All right, you can have it for twenty-five, but not for less."

Fritz pulled out the money and handed Kaufmann thirty rubels.

"Don't you have even money?" Kaufmann seemed reluctant to give back the proper change. When Fritz denied having change, Kaufmann tried to make him go back to his barracks for it. But Fritz insisted that he make change on the spot.

Kaufmann was obviously upset. Finally he pulled out a purse which he wore on a string fastened around his neck. He always kept his money under his shirt, as this was the safest place. When Fritz saw the rubel bills stuffed into the purse, his eyes brightened. We all were surprised that a prisoner could amass such a large amount of money. Kaufmann was chagrined; he had been forced to expose his hiding place to Fritz.

Several nights later I was having trouble trying to get to sleep. I had not earned much that month and I was hungry; and the hunger was keeping me awake. Every once in awhile a prisoner would get up and go to the toilet. To fill our stomachs, we were all drinking too much water again. Suddenly I saw a shadow steal past my bunk, but I didn't pay much attention. Kaufmann was snoring as usual. After a while the snores ceased; he muttered in his sleep and turned over. About then the shadow went silently past my bunk and left through the door. His silhouette looked like Fritz, but I knew he wasn't among the thirty or so men who slept in our barracks.

I didn't really care what he was doing there. Somehow I fell asleep.

Early in the morning, Kaufmann was up shouting, "Someone stole my money!"

I opened my eyes and realized I must have slept. Kaufmann was sitting on his bunk cursing. His vituperative language boiled down to the fact that his money was gone and he didn't know who had stolen it.

"I'm going to strangle him," he threatened. "He won't get out of this room alive."

I rolled back my blanket and walked over to his bunk where several others were gathered. Kaufmann was breathless and could hardly talk now.

"Look at this!" He pointed toward a slash in his shirt. He pulled the material apart, and there was an empty purse dangling from the neck. Someone had cut his shirt with a knife and stolen his money.

"How much did you lose?" I inquired.

"About seven hundred rubels. Can you imagine that?"

"Seven hundred rubels." A man repeated the figure.

"Seven hundred rubels! What a fortune!"

"It wasn't us," someone said.

"Well, if it was nobody in this barracks, who do you think it was?" Kaufmann wanted to know.

"Until a few days ago when you gave Fritz back that change, I didn't even know you had so much money."

"What did you say about Fritz? I bet it was he!" Kaufmann was almost ready to jump up and run to the barracks where Fritz lived.

I discouraged him from accusing Fritz in person. "He probably hid it and besides—" Fritz was about twenty-five years old, six feet tall, and strong as a bear. Kaufmann was over fifty and, although strong otherwise, he had always been troubled by his legs. In addition, Fritz was a Russian citizen depite his present status and he had many friends. In the days that followed, Fritz did not act differently than he had before the robbery. However, after a while it was noticeable that he was eating better. In a few weeks he was sent to another camp. Either he was able to bribe his transfer with his new money or the administration was on to his tricks.

I happened to see Kaufmann one day after Fritz had left and I casually asked him: "What were you going to do with all that money anyway?"

"You might not believe it, but I was saving the money to buy a bakery when I'm released." He was an unfailing optimist to be even planning ahead. Most of us lived just for the present day.

INDOCTRINATION

In spite of all the propaganda effort, we remained relatively immune to the Communistic doctrines. There was never any Communistic cell within our camp. Our anti-Communist attitude was unusual since most of the other POW camps had been somewhat proselyted.

We received newspapers from the "Committee of Free Germany," an organization of German POW's who had become Communists. Some of these articles made me more of a patriot than before. It was specially interesting to follow the different newspaper articles which discussed life in Western capitalistic countries. The Russian government did not present objective news; the achievements of the Western Allies were hardly reported.

We often debated issues of minor importance and, if a few of our own fellows or the Russians used swear words in speaking of Germany, we stood together as a whole in opposing them. The contrast between Russia and other Western nations was obvious to us. Russia offered the individual little hope; in regard to spiritual concerns, nothing was presented. The state was the only god allowed.

One day the children of one of the Russian officials went with me to get some hay for the cattle. One took along a schoolbook. I paged inquisitively through it till I came to a picture of German soldiers led by a boy with a flute. With my imagination I was able to fill in the meaning of the picture, which illustrated how a boy, perhaps of the guerilla army, led a company of German soldiers into a trap something like a modern Pied Piper of Hamelin.

"Father" Stalin, who previously had been photographed in a plain linen jacket, had been advanced to the rank of marshall of the Soviet Union and had been decorated with many colorful medals. His picture and those of other Soviet officials were on practically all official buildings. Any Russian who compared the circumstances before the October Revolution of 1917 to those which prevailed afterward, could easily see the drastic changes without much propaganda. My father had often said that war spoils the people. I asked myself if a whole philosophy had not ruined the Russians.

13

A NEW ERA

The administration of the Solchose was divided into various sections. At the head of all was the *Natschailnic*. Under him were the work chief who was responsible for the general work; a coordination chief; a chief of the guard who checked up on the field watchmen; a chief responsible for the oxen and horse barn; and a food chief who rationed out both the feed for animals and the groceries. In charge of the camp was a commander. The *agronom* was the overseer of the ground farming and distributed the right plant food for the field crops. The chief gardener managed to raise cucumbers in glass hothouses— quite an achievement for such a northern country.

Among the ten officers working in the bureau were the chief bookkeeper, the cashier, and a man who was something like a union boss, although no union exists in Russia. One man took care of the feed mill and the cabbage barn.

The baker and his two helpers baked the bread and sent it to the Russians and ration-card owners among the prisoners. In the work-brigade kitchen, five people were employed.

The hospital kitchen had three workers. A chief doctor was head of the hospital, which had facilities for 150 people, while a brigade doctor served the working brigades. Besides that, a medical man was in charge of the bath and the disinfection station.

Everything was carefully divided. The brigades were separated into groups of four with one man in charge. And of course there was always a supervisor in charge of those who were in charge.

The specialists belonged to a special organization. The lumberyard supervisor was over fifteen workers. The wood brigadier was responsible for cutting and dividing the wood. The tractor brigade included truck and caterpillar drivers, mechanics and technicians who worked day and night shifts, as did a gang of technicians at the electric plant. A shift commonly lasted twelve hours.

The electric plant consisted of a mobile steam engine which ran a dynamo and was cared for by an engineer and a fireman. The carpenter brigade of eight people repaired the camp buildings in summertime and set up new buildings in wintertime, when the wood was easier to work with. Two men in the tool shop distributed the tools in the morning to the outgoing brigades and checked them in in the evening. In the meantime they repaired broken tools.

There were officials, officials and more officials. Since there were more of them than necessary, and since they did not work very much but received comparatively high incomes, the *Solchose* was deep in debt. Later they tried to cancel the debt by inventing the clever idea of making us pay for the camp clothing we had received eighteen months earlier, which was in most cases completely worn-out. This injustice forced many prisoners to steal from their own comrades as well as from the Russians.

Advantages and Disadvantages

I enjoyed a comparatively better time in the period between October and November, 1946. We had to work very hard but at least my job paid well. I became a driver of an oxen team which hauled water. The improvement was that this time I had the best oxen on the farm; however, this did not mean that I never had any trouble. When I was filling the barrels I could not avoid spilling some water. Since the temperature stayed at five to fifteen degrees below zero, the water froze instantly. After I had suffered a frozen toe I remembered to fill the barrel instead of my shoe. The effects of that cold weather would plague me years later.

The blizzards in that northern country were especially severe. I remember one day when I could see only about twenty yards ahead. I had to go out with the oxen team whether I wanted to or not since the cattle needed water. The track was invisible and the snowbanks became higher and higher. There was hardly any way to get around the oncoming sled traffic; it was extremely dangerous to get out of the track and to get stuck, even with empty water barrels. Since the snow was five to six feet deep I tried to drag out some of the water sleds which had become stuck and had been abandoned by the drivers and their teams. But I did not have much luck, for the barrels were half frozen inside and the dipper with which I filled the barrels became heavier and heavier because of the thickening coat of ice. Besides that, the oxen did not cooperate that day. They missed the track and turned the whole load over into the snow.

My monthly income was about 300 rubles, worth about 150 dollars, and I was one of the best-paid workers on the *Solchose*. The food I received for my ration cards was now adequate since we also received some extra food at the hog kitchen. I even was able to sell some of my coupons in contrast to former times when I was forced to buy some myself. My greatest dream was to get a pair of felt boots which I would need very badly for the water transport. My problem was that I didn't know where I could get them. The fellows in the camp did not have any, and on the free market they were tremendously expensive. The only access to them might be to look up the *Sacluschoni*; they were Russian and

171

Polish prisoners who shared the camp with us and who might take a risk of selling a pair of newly acquired boots. Their boots looked very appropriate to me. But since I did not find the right size, I bought myself a pair of fur gloves and a woolen undershirt for fifty rubles.

Soon afterward the food became very expensive, probably because of the crop failure in the Ukraine. The quality of the goods improved, but the price went up accordingly. In those winter months we discovered for the first time that candy and chocolate could be bought instead of sugar.

In the stores we frequently felt the hatred of the Russians for the Germans. Prejudice was obvious when twenty Germans would wait their turn for hours, but newly arrived Russians could step through the crowd and receive service at once. Quite often some of the prisoners lost their tempers; such treatment usually resulted in very heated arguments, to say the least.

GLIMPSE OF HOPE

One evening I was among those given the special job of getting the bedbugs out of the furniture being used by one of the officials. We carried the furniture to the hog kitchen in order to scald the joints with hot water. As we sat in the light of a dim lamp waiting until the water was hot enough, Mrs. Koch, the wife of the camp official, looked considerately toward me and asked how old I was.

When I told her that I was seventeen, she shook her head and made a remark that I would be going home soon. I desperately wanted to believe her, and in the following days I often thought of her words. I wondered: *Can it be true that we really will be able to go home? Can it be true that the Russians will release us?* Day and night I was haunted by the possibility. During the night I lay awake wondering if it would soon be over. Some were tossing in their beds, others perhaps were praying—all of us with the same idea of freedom. But when morning came it was all the same again; nothing had changed. Discouraged, we walked to our various jobs. Many of us had given up hope. There was nothing we could do. It didn't make any difference if we were on our good behavior or not.

On the other hand, without our noticing it we had slowly become adjusted to the Russian culture and environment. We often spoke Russian even among ourselves; for some words we no longer tried to think of the German equivalent. To express ourselves we even cursed with profane Russian swear words.

One morning the cook in the hog kitchen told me that all Germans were to be released! The news swept through the camp like a prairie fire. We did not know whether we should laugh or weep. We flung our arms around each other in joy. I had never experienced such great happiness.

After this announcement we did our work more quickly than ever before. A few prisoners did not believe the statement was true. But soon the official announcement came: we were to leave in one week!

Even before the news came, we had noticed that the key jobs—those with special privileges—were being given to Russian prisoners. The Russians worked according to the probation system: if a criminal had been sentenced for five years in the northern districts he could be turned loose if he behaved, but he had to remain within the prison colony. There was no chance to escape. Attempted escape was suicide. The only traffic line was the railroad which was continually controlled by an immense police force. Some tried it once in a while but most got caught a few miles away from the camp, only to be shipped to a camp where there were fewer privileges and harsher treatment. With little knowledge of the language and with no money, flight was impossible anyway for us Germans.

The other driver and I were the last persons from our group to work officially for the camp. At last the unbelievable came to pass; we were officially discharged and paid our final wages. I received 270 rubles for twenty-one days of work. My feelings were so confused that little else mattered but my coming freedom. I had all but given up hope that whatever Providence there might be was watching over me.

Till the arrival of the boxcars for our transportation, we were supposed to continue our work for payment in kind. We labored three days but didn't get anything. After a short argument with the brigadier, I quit and went to saw wood for the civilians, who gave each of us three rubles and three pounds of oatmeal for two hours of work. This extra earning helped to provide for us until we left.

Fellowship among us Germans had improved tremendously since learning that we would soon be allowed to leave. We sat on our beds around the stove until late at night talking about home and all the familiar places where we had had such a good life without realizing it.

In those days prior to our departure, and even on our trip, we wondered continually about one thing: *What had happened to our homes? Would we be able to return home again? Would the people from East and West Prussia be able to find a dwelling place in one of the four occupation zones? Who was occupying East Prussia—the Poles or the Russians?* And then the biggest question was: *Where are our relatives? Are they still living, or are they all in Russia now too?*

PREPARATION FOR RELEASE

The day came—November 27, 1946—that we had longed for since the day we had arrived. We knew it was final when the unmistakable order was given: "All camp-owned property is to be turned in." I forgot my case against the fate which had allowed me to suffer as I had. Now I was thankful for a merciful destiny. I put my old blanket into the pile of goods being turned in. With caution I kept the new camp blanket we had received just a few weeks before. It was not easy saying good-bye to my old blanket; it had been with me

174

for two years and we had become good friends. That blanket had kept me warm and, in turn, I had tried to keep it properly repaired. For two years my blanket had been my closet companion, one who never argued with me nor complained, but had always been willing to render sacrificial service unto me. The blanket was badly worn out. The sub-zero weather where I had been living, close to the Arctic Circle, had necessitated constant use. We all had hoped the Russians might give us new clothing for propaganda reasons; but our speculations proved to be in vain. Although I knew in my mind that the blanket had outlived its usefulness, my heart belied my reason. I had become attached to the blanket, the only comfort I had had over the years. But I turned it in and kept the newer, less-sentimental one.

On November 28 we were given final orders: "Get ready to leave!" Although we wanted to rush out, we knew we had to be cautious. We wanted to observe firsthand the searching procedures of the various camp guards. Still suspicious, we wanted to know where it would be easiest to get through. Prisoners were searched before being allowed to leave as an effort to keep everything in the camp which the state owned, for it was natural that the prisoners would try to take along as much as possible. In order to find out how the Russians went about this duty, we sent observers to the camp gate. They were to find out which guards were conscientious and which were less thorough, and where it was easiest to get through inspection with the least losses. Soon we received the first news from the front lines, as we facetiously called the last guards between us and the outside of the camp. The guards were opening everything: cereal sacks, knapsacks, satchels and suitcases. The most careful and thorough of them all were the women guards of the NKWD. After our observers had told us where it was easiest to get through, we adjusted our plans accordingly. I rolled my blanket around my body and then put on my Russian army topcoat. Then I wound a rope around my waist—

which prisoners often did—to make my form look more natural and not to arouse the guards' curiosity. Finally my turn came. Approaching a guard who I'd been told was not quite so strict, I looked as innocent as I could and opened my baggage for examination. After it was searched, I was pronounced as being OK and allowed to go through without losses.

Next we had to march about one and a half miles to the station while our baggage was taken there by sleds. The boxcars were waiting; they looked like the same ones in which we had traveled to this country. It was the standard method of transporting prisoners and judged sufficient to take us away.

Again the boxcar was heated by a small stove. But this time there was wood provided for us to burn; it had been contributed by the *Solchose*—our final gift from that institution. Fortunately it was not terribly cold, only three degrees below zero. Being accustomed to much lower temperatures, we did not suffer as we waited inside the boxcar.

Going Home

During the night the locomotive came. Everybody was lying quietly in our boxcar, although nobody slept. Finally the engine was successfully attached to the train and we started moving. We felt it was really a historical event. There was joy unspeakable among us. At that point it was as much of heaven on earth as I had known.

Click—click—click—click—click—click— With a rattling of the wheels the locomotive got underway. There was a difference in our tolerance of the now-familiar musical background to our thoughts. A new note in their monotonous grinding could be heard: *Home—home—we are going home!*

In the beginning our boxcars were usually hooked onto freight trains. But the further south we went, the more of our former original transport was picked up along the way. Or rather, the remainder of that transport was picked up

176

again. Later we became an independent train, although this train was not even half as long as the one on which we had come. A Russian GPU lieutenant was the train's commander, and his helper was the food administrator. These men were unique in that they both were excellent profiteers. The first part of our trip went fairly well as far as money and food supplies were concerned. Everybody was in an excellent mood. We sang a great deal, touching on old folk songs, national songs and even the national anthem. Everybody had something uplifting to contribute to the conversation. Old familiar stories were retold, spirits were high. The little stove was cluttered with cooking pots. Others of the group sat in the door, reveled in the beauty of nature, and made comments about everything, beginning with the observation that we were going further south, and extending to the description of what food they would eat first on arriving home.

The landscape was almost always the same; we went by large virgin forests, swamps, abandoned camps and, every fifteen miles, a depot. The abandoned camps were built in a very primitive fashion. Each of them undoubtedly would be able to tell a story which would overshadow any of our experiences. The camps did not speak to us, but the sight of their primitive twisted fences pressed toward heaven, and the empty window frames, gazing at us like skulls, was depressing. We identified with the unspoken misery they represented. Perhaps right behind the hill between those stumps were the mass graves, meaningless to their Communistic government, and there was the old watchtower on which the guard had pulled the trigger to finish the life of someone who, in his despair, tried to escape. Our minds were in limbo, still in the grips of the horrifying experience not yet behind us. The future ahead of us was still not real and not coming into realization fast enough.

RETURN BY TRAIN

Once we stopped somewhere on the tracks between two

depots. Sixty men were called out. They took their baggage and went along with some officials. We learned that they were being taken to another camp. This was quite a shock to us. We had thought we were on our way home. The Russians explained that the men would have to stay there as "specialists" until the other prisoners would be able to take over the jobs.

We had learned in the past how long some of these temporary periods could be. Once they had taken me for only six days to feed cows, and this time had been prolonged into two years. The men who were called were from the second category; they were the strongest among us. In one case a father was in the second category and his son was in the third category. They had managed to stay together for these two years; now they were separated on the basis of this heartless division. It is this kind of unfeeling authority that the practice of Communism breeds. The individual is never considered.

In Kottlas, the largest city of the Komi-SSR, our train had to undergo a strict police control. A whole army of officers with bloodhounds checked our train. We were counted more than once. The guards even looked under the train to see whether there were any extra people hiding there. A favorite stowaway trick was to hide between the axles of the boxcar and the platform. Also we learned that the city of Komi was the main checking point for all upgoing and downgoing traffic. Anyone who managed to get through the tight security there without being caught was pretty safe.

One day I sat with Horst Schremer in the open door of the boxcar and looked at the passing scenery. Click— click—click—each turn of the wheels brought us closer home. Click—click—click, each turn of the wheels was music in our ears.

"What will you do when you get home, Horst?" I asked conversationally.

"I would like to work in my trade," he answered. "How-

178

ever, I wonder whether it wouldn't be better to work on a farm."

"You're quite right, at least there you would get enough to eat."

"What are you going to do?" he asked.

"Well, when I was a boy, I wanted to be a general," I said. "But having seen war like this has made me change my mind. Perhaps I'll try the farm too."

"What do you think you can make there?" he asked.

"Well, I never thought about that part of it. We have been so hungry here that I will be happy if only I have enough to eat for the rest of my life."

"But what about clothing?"

"I don't think I'll ever care too much about that," I said. "The main thing I am yearning for is to always have a full stomach."

"And drink as much as I want," he added. "But where will you go? Didn't you have a nice farm?"

"Don't remind me," I said. "It makes me cry to think of it."

"You think your parents are still living?" he asked.

"Well, I told you that they displaced my father. He is probably dead, judging by what they made us endure, and I don't know whether they arrested my mother too."

"Would you like to go home—that is, where you once lived?"

"No," I replied. "I've lived long enough under foreigners now. I would like to be with people that talk my language again and think the way I do and, most of all, people who aren't Communist exploiters."

"Well, you know that the Russians have occupied Eastern Germany?"

"Yes," I said, "I know that. Perhaps we can request them to discharge us to West Germany, perhaps to the American Zone."

"Request," he joked. "You know how much you can request from the Soviets."

179

The sun had gone down in the meantime. A chilly wind blew from the east. We got up and shut the door in order to keep the little warmth we had inside the boxcar.

14

RETURN TICKET

Our train went on to Welikiji-Ustjuki, and from there to Moscow. When our food rations became shorter and I ran out of money, I sold my blanket for sixty rubles to buy some bread. At that time bread was fifteen rubles a pound. Although it was very cold, I tried to get along with my topcoat.

Often the Russians had little markets set up beside the railroad tracks at the train depots. One of the favorite dishes they sold to the passing prisoners or Russians was pancakes. Of course we were always hungry and were always out for the most for the least money. We always looked for the biggest pancakes, and the Russians must have caught on to what we were doing, for they began fitting their merchandise to our needs. It became their favorite trick to fill these pancakes with something besides dough. It was usually too late by the time we realized we had been tricked; the pancakes had been sold out and the salesman was gone. Quite distinctly I remember innocently buying pancakes, only to find them filled with sauerkraut. We had been eating sauerkraut for two years and were not particularly anxious to eat more. After we finally found out what it was all about, we were out of money.

Shortly before we arrived at Moscow our steam engine was replaced by an electric engine. We rolled into the capital of the Union of Socialistic Soviet Republics in modern locomotion. Everybody pushed to the door to get a glimpse of the city. We had been here before, but it was during the night and behind closed doors or in the disinfecting shower room. We scarcely remembered anything about that city. This time we could see a little more and were more interested.

The outskirts of the city were mostly made up of very fine wooden houses, it was a parkline section. The main city was composed mostly of one-story buildings which were arranged in city blocks. The wide streets and alleys and the many squares impressed me most.

Where the railroad tracks intersected the shopping centers and the busier places of the city, the street scenery was dominated by the uniforms of civil officers and army officers. The people generally were dressed a little better than those I had seen in other parts of Russia, but hats, ties and other Western articles of clothing were not seen frequently. The women wore scarfs or veils and usually were dressed modestly. The men wore fur caps when they weren't wearing an officer's cap to match their uniform. Matters of dress often presented a paradox. A typical Russian costume might be supplemented by a piece of clothing of Western origin, probably imported by plundering soldiers from Germany or other occupied countries which had some way or other become the spoils of the victorious revolution.

The traffic of the cars on the street moved rapidly. But the public conveyances were so overcrowded that people clustered around the steps in order to get a ride. It was also interesting to observe the methods of street cleaning, for women usually were assigned to that work.

Russia has a law that prohibits nude statues in parks;

therefore the figures are at least dressed in bathing suits. Most of the Russian women had not cut their hair nor did they wear lipstick.

As a whole the Russian people we observed in Moscow looked healthy and well cared for. One of the other interesting observations of that day concerned an old cathedral with its big onion towers; it stood as a reminder of the once-progressive church in Russia. Today it is a testimony to the world of a church which became cold and indifferent. When the church did not have much to offer to the people, they became an easy prey for godless Communism.

MOSCOW TO BREST-LITOVSK

It had taken us two weeks to reach Moscow. The food was now becoming worse and worse, probably because the train commander and his food chief had peddled some of our food to other people along the way and had filled their own pockets with the money. Our hope that the free-market price for bread and other foodstuffs would be lower further south was not realized. Instead, the price went up.

The train went on, passing forests, swamps, little towns, former trenches and old bunkers, burned-out tanks and other things which reminded us of former battles. Little graves here and there witnessed to the enormous losses of those battles. These graves were only a few of the millions that were scattered all over the world as a result of the war. About 6.6 million Germans had been killed, a large percentage of them in Russia. According to a report released in 1953, there were 1.2 million Germans still missing in Russia. Besides that, perhaps millions of civilians were missing in the East. Russia lost, according to this report, twenty million soldiers and civilians.*

Our next temporary destination was Brest-Litovsk, a large

---

* *Deutschland Heute,* published by the press and Information Bureau of the Federal Republic of West Germany.

183

city just inside the Russian border. It has a large railroad yard. Since Russia uses broad-gauge railroad tracks, and the other European countries use standard gauge, everything needed to be unloaded and reloaded at this border station. Our train moved along the wide track beside another train parked on a normal track. Then we had to transfer to the other train.

Shortly before reaching this city we lost one fellow, Horst Fischer. Although he was still young, Horst liked to smoke. We had run out of water in our boxcar and no one had felt like getting more because there was no well close to the place where the train had stopped. Knowing Horst's habit, some of the fellows offered him a cigarette if he would go and get a pail of water. After short negotiations, he grabbed the pail and went.

Before long, the train blew the whistle and started moving. Horst had not come back. We didn't know what had happened to him—whether the police had picked him up and sent him back to the camp where we had come from or whether they had sent him on with the next transport. We never found out. Perhaps the difference between slavery in Russia or freedom in Germany depended upon this one cigarette.

We were rolling toward the Polish border. Our train commander, against government orders, had shortened our bread rations from day to day. Now he conceived a new method by which he could get even more money out of us. When we approached the Polish border he told us that the Poles would not let us pass the border unless each of us paid them one ruble.

Now one ruble is not very much if there are more where that came from. But since 90 percent of us were out of money, we were forced to pay with our ration of bread, a scarce commodity. We gave our bread to the guard who supposedly paid the commander with money, thus allowing us to cross the border. But we all suspected that he actually pocketed those seven hundred rubles himself. But since no-body really knew what had happened, all we could do was to pull in our belts one hole tighter and keep looking ahead.

STRAINED RELATIONS

The insufficient food and the extended period of time on the trip—which had already lasted three weeks—brought a return of hostility among us which increased daily. Little fights became more and more frequent, and arguments occurred often. One day when I was standing close to the door watching the scenery outside, the supervisor of our boxcar wanted to stand where I was. Because of his roughness and his ability to work fast, he had been promoted to a brigadier while we were in camp. Since I did not move quickly enough to suit him, he slapped me across the face so hard that I saw stars. I became hot and cold in my anger to retaliate, but I decided it would be better to practice self-control.

It was one of the hardest things I ever did. But I remembered that in the camp the same man had once ran after another fellow with a bread knife. And I am convinced that if he had caught the other fellow while his temper was boiling, he would have used that knife. This was not the only case of violence. Thinking about all this in about one second's time I decided to retreat; saying nothing, I crawled into my corner like a licked dog. By fighting I would have gained nothing, but it was hard not to return the insult.

The scenery changed rapidly after we had crossed the Polish border. Earlier in Russia I had seen a few bicycles; in Poland almost everybody seemed to be riding them. There was an aura of trade and happiness over Poland. It astonished us that the Polish people had recuperated so fast after the war.

Soon our train came to the Polish capital of Warsaw. Here the wounds of the last conflict had not yet been completely healed. In some places at least two hundred destroyed tanks were lined up in a field. The houses showed the results of

185

extreme fighting, the marks of exploding bombs, shells, rifle, and machine-gun fire. The last fighting must have been terrible.

Stopping at the Warsaw railroad yard, we saw a train with returning Russian soldiers on the opposite track. After the manner of returning conquerors, their boxcars were filled with beds, radios, bicycles, and clothing which had been taken along as spoils by the "liberators." Some had civilian suits on under their uniforms. Gradually we got into conversation with them; some even came over to our train to talk. They seemed interested in talking with us than with the Poles. It soon became obvious that most of them weren't too happy about their return, even though they were on their way to their so-called paradise. They knew that modern conveniences like electric lights and running water, which they had been enjoying in European countries, would not be available to them in Russia. In their ignorance, the Russians had often used toilet bowls as washbasins. Our conversation also revealed that some had comforted themselves with the idea that they would soon be in America or England. They were looking forward to the girls there. One drunken tank soldier said with a smile, "Now that we know the German girls, we would like to see the American and English girls."

ALMOST LEFT BEHIND

In Warsaw I amost had the same fate as that of Horst Fischer. An older man and I were sawing wood for our furnace. Meanwhile my fellow prisoners in the boxcar had observed that the Russians had accidently dumped a sack of starch while reloading some foodstuffs. Some of the fellows had already gone over and helped themselves to the spilled potato flour. Since we had to saw wood we went on with our work, but when it was done we rushed over to gather up the flour. Although there wasn't much left except some mixed with cinders, we tried to pick up the best and then rushed back toward the train. By that time it had become dark; only random lights brightened up the railroad yard. A few locomotives were moving about and we could see some red and white signal lamps.

About fifty yards away, two red lights began moving away from us. It suddenly dawned on me that these must be the taillights of our train. We started to run as if we were racing for our lives. The train moved faster and faster. We tried to run faster too, at the same time trying to hold onto the sack of starch. It was harder and harder for us to run as we became more exhausted. Ahead of us our train was moving on. My buddy, an older man of forty-eight, was only a few steps behind me. "Jump onto the bumpers," he said with an effort, puffing with the exertion. Even though we were quite close to them, a feeling of apprehension gripped me. *The temperature is near zero today,* I thought. *We're sweaty from the long run, and we don't know how soon the train will stop again.*

In a last desperate effort to get on the train, I moved ahead and grabbed the handle of the door of the last car and pulled myself up—I was safe! My buddy ran ahead further and grabbed the next car handle. After I had caught my breath, although I did not believe much in God at that time, I breathed a prayer to Him and thanked Him for that moment. Somehow I realized I had not done the impossible by myself. I looked around in the boxcar; I was its lone occupant. Because it was dark and cold and chills were creeping up my back, I started to do gymnastics and to run from one end of the car to the other. The train kept moving. It was at least two hours before we reached a large railroad yard and our train really stopped. How thankful we were that we had not jumped on the bumpers and perhaps been frozen to death! We walked up along the other boxcars till we finally reached our own. Our buddies had not expected to see us again after the train left without us. We were happy to be reunited again, and relieved not to have met the fate of Horst Fischer.

Another incident happened in Poland. Even though Poland had annexed upper Silesia, it did not have much coal;

187

therefore, the price of coal was very high. Evidently the engineer of our train, a German, had sold some coal to civilians along the way for a high black-market price. When we arrived in another city, the Poles checked the coal supply and arrested our engineer for selling the coal. This delayed our return for another day. But eventually another steam engine was attached to our train and we moved along toward home.

FINAL IMPRISONMENT

The hope we had cherished to be home for Christmas was not fulfilled. We had found out that we would not be returning to East or West Prussia but would be discharged in Frankfurt at the Oder. On the morning of December 24 we rode over the Oder bridge. For us it was an historical moment when we crossed the river and arrived once more in German territory. Here we were reminded of the fact that Germany was a defeated nation. Our train stopped beside an army camp loaded with Russian soldiers. After an interval, the train moved on to another camp. Finally we were discharged from the train and marched off two by two. Without fanfare, the moment of our release was near, but there was no letdown by the guards in their authority over us. We were counted again and again. The Russians were apparently anxious that our number had not increased. Then we were marched to an old German army camp and left for a short time in a large room. There was work for us to do here and we carried out orders of sawing wood and completing other jobs. The next day we learned that our train commander and the food manager had been arrested under the suspicion of wrongdoing. But this action was too late to benefit us.

Our camp was divided into two parts by six fences of barbed wire. One half was for us and was only lightly guarded, but the other side was watched more carefully. A policeman said the prisoners in the other half were mainly former Nazi officials, officers, and factory owners.

In the evening we had to haul food to these prisoners—a job which we actually appreciated because it gave us a chance to eat a little bit on the side; even at this time most of our thoughts and affections were centered upon food. First we pulled two trailers over to the storage room about a mile away from the army camp. When we returned to the camp we watched ourselves very carefully at the gate to the more heavily guarded prison so that we would not be trapped in the line into the other camp. At the gate we gave the trailer a push and let it roll over into the other yard where it was received by the other prisoners. We avoided any contact with them.

RELEASE CERTIFICATE

On Christmas Day, 1946, my buddies and I were closely checked to see if we had any mail from German prisoners in Russia that we were trying to smuggle through. Several of us had received letters while our train was stopped at several places in Russia where we had been brought into contact with other German prisoners. I remember quite well that the Christian pastor had a letter to Frankfurt/Main in Germany which he had received from one of the prisoners. All this mail was taken away from us. After all these matters were attended to, we were officially released from the Russians and were given a certificate of release. It was only a piece of paper, but its significance to me was inexpressible. I carefully put it in my pocket—it was the passport to a life of my own. I still carry it with me.

Only one who has been a prisoner can imagine the joy with which we received our freedom from the Russians. But this first joy was somewhat dampened by the two weeks it took to complete the details of our discharge. First there was another train ride to Gronenfelde near Frankfurt/Oder. We remained there for two days, then took another train to another camp, and still another to Altengurg. Here we had a physical examination while our clothing was disinfected in a hot oven to prevent us from taking any insect residents along with us into private life.

From there we were taken to a quarantine camp in Thuringia, and again checked for various diseases. The camp administration promised us new clothing, but we did not receive any. Later we learned that the county administrator had left for West Germany with about one million marks; apparently our clothing money went with him. He had been one of the most powerful Communists in that territory, but he moved on when it seemed that his wrongdoings were to be discovered.

What can I do now? I wondered. The future was uncertain. *What has happened to my relatives? What has happened to our possessions? What has happened to all the people in the east? Are they still at home? Are they already on the west side of the Oder-Neisse line?** *Or have they also been displaced to the east?* All these speculations went through my mind.

Because of insufficient food in camp, we were forced to beg for food in nearby villages. Since we still wore Russian clothing, the people often thought we were Russians. Sometimes they slammed and locked the door as soon as they saw us. Once when we came to a house an old grandfather started speaking to us in sign language, supposing we were Russians and could not understand German. He was very surprised when he heard us speak the German language.

With our fur caps, our Russian soldier shirts, our steppe pants, our Russian military topcoats, our Russian boots, even with our Russian short crew haircuts, we really looked like Russians. Besides that, our faces were swollen from drinking too much water.

It was very humiliating for me, having been raised on the farm of a fairly well-to-do farmer, to go around and beg from those small farmers in the mountains of Thuringia. Often during the night I lay awake and meditated on this situation, deciding not to beg again; but when the morning came and

---

* This became the borderline between Germany and Poland after 1945. This line cut off the former East-German provinces from the Reich.

hunger returned, I got my rucksack and went begging once more. I often remembered the words my father had spoken to me in my childhood: "The crust you are now throwing away you might have to seek sometime."

I realized now that I had returned to Germany I was faced with the task of finding a suitable occupation. My youthful ambition to become an officer in the army had been frustrated—not only by disillusionment but also by the fact that there was no army. The idea of going into a professional field or of acquiring an education was hindered by the inadequate food situation in the cities. All that was left for me was to follow the occupation of my father: farming. I would have to help a farmer as a farmhand; I could not expect high wages, but at least I'd get sufficient food and clothing. I had learned to be content with the essentials of life.

During my time in the quarantine camp I quite frequently visited a nearby farmer. While eating dinner there one Sunday, he asked me what I would do after I was released from the camp. He mentioned that he needed extra help and would be glad to have me work for him. So after my time in the camp, I became his farmhand.

It took me quite a while to adjust myself to the German culture again. During the time we had been in Russia we had forgotten part of our language and practically all of our manners, and had become clumsy in everything we did. Walking nine months of the year in the snow had changed our manner of walking and our whole way of doing things. Quite frequently I used Russian curse words while tending the cows. Another former prisoner worked with me, and he too caught himself cursing the cows in Russian. Later on we both changed to cursing in German.

About 50 yards away from us we saw two red lights moving down the tracks. In a last desperate effort to board the train, I moved ahead and grabbed the handle of the door of the last car and pulled myself up—safe!

Drawing: Jan Gleysteen

15

ADJUSTMENTS

After I had worked for this farmer for about eight weeks I was called by the county administration to help dismantle factories for the Russians. My employer, the farmer, was a former Nazi official and during the war had been the town mayor. Now the Russians wanted him to do some work for them as punishment for his Nazi connections, having imprisoned him already two years before that. Two other farmers in that village who had been Nazis were also required to dismantle factories or to send a substitute. My boss sent me as his substitute.

My feelings were mixed about this development. I thought it was unjust of him to send me since I had just recently been released by the Russians. On the other hand, I did not feel that my boss should have gone since he had a family. As far as politics were concerned, we both agreed, having both been early indoctrinated with the Nazi doctrines. With other Germans I was taken to Leipzig, where we dismantled the brown-coal processing works of Regis-Breitingen, a factory in the Saxon brown-coal district. My patience was almost gone. I was altogether unable to like this job, for with our work we were making other people jobless.

Being very unhappy with this situation, I decided to go back to the farm. But after being with the farmer only a few days, I found that I would be forced to return to the factory. So I went over to the employment office which was run by the Communistic government and asked them the reason why I always had to work for the Russians. There were other people who had never worked for the Russians, and I wondered why they did not take them. We talked back and forth, till finally the Communist officer told me that I would be released if I would provide a substitute. Since I was unable to do that, I had to go myself again.

I was even more disgusted, but I returned. After working there for a few more weeks with very little interest, especially since the food was quite insufficient, I decided to desert again. But it was hard to get away from there for now one needed a traveling permit. That area was jammed with workers being forced to dismantle factories and many of the dissatisfied people had already left. It was finally decreed that nobody could buy a ticket to a distant point without traveling permission.

We found out that in the smaller railroad depots outside the big cities it was possible to receive traveling permits without many complications. One day I traveled to a small village by train and lied to the depot administrator; he believed me and gave me a permit. I was able to obtain a ticket and go home again to my old boss on the farm. This time I had decided that if the situation would become too bad, I would go over to the Western Zone.

Meanwhile I had written to my relatives and found out that my mother was still living, together with my three younger brothers, in East Prussia. I also had found out that one of my uncles was living in West Germany. My mother wrote that Father, after being displaced in 1945, had never returned.

Sometime later I found out the following story about Father: Two weeks after I had been taken captive, one of our former milk-testers who had been taken with Father to a camp in East Prussia. At that time Father was already sixty-three years of age and in such poor health that he had been discharged from the army. And if the German army discharged someone, that meant he was really sick. Because of insufficient food and clothing, old age and rough treatment, Father had become terribly ill. He gave the milk-tester a message for us in case he was released. My mother was to be told that if my father did not return within six days that his grave would most likely be somewhere in the vicinity of two certain East German cities. The milk-tester was released from the camp and came home with the news. But Father never returned. My worst fears had been confirmed, and my sense of loss was deep.

I also had a brother who had been in the German army, fighting in East Prussia during the Russian offensive. His fate was never known to us; he never came back either. There were two main possibilities: either he was killed in battle or taken prisoner and shipped to Russia.

My mother and my brothers had been taken from our farm and put on another farm to work. Some of our former Polish workers had told the Polish National Guard that Father had formerly been an army captain, and that he had been a former concentration-camp commander. Although the latter was never true, it was hard to prove. Mother had become ill with typhoid fever at the farm where she was working. She was still sick in bed when one of the men who had been working for us and who had in the meantime been promoted to lieutenant in the Polish National Guard came to arrest her since they could not find Father. He told her that he would wait till she was well again. After Mother had recovered from the fever, he came and arrested her, putting her into the Elbing prison.

FREEDOM

I was always very much interested in the political life of our nation and of our village. One evening when my boss invited me to a session of the village council which was held in one of the guesthouses there, I gladly went along. Before the session started, the village mayor called my boss outside to talk with him alone. When both returned after about ten minutes, my boss looked toward me with a strange expression on his face. In the beginning I did not think much about it and was talking with the other young people there. The session began and they discussed the new village water system among other things. We drank some shale beer and the farmers went on to talk about a community project of planting a common orchard.

Suddenly the door opened and Maria, a hired refugee girl from Bohemia who worked on our farm, motioned to me: "Come here!" she whispered.

I thought she was joking and stayed where I was. But she got so excited that I finally went to her.

"Listen," she said, "the village mayor just received a phone call ordering him to ship you as soon as possible to the county seat. It has been found out at the county work administration that you have deserted that dismantling place near Leipzig."

Slowly I walked back to my table. I had not yet paid for the beer. My boss leaned over to me and asked what was wrong. I told him: "They're looking for me. This time I won't be here. I'm going to run."

He nodded in agreement and said I could go right away.

But I knew I could not go then. I had just worked about fourteen hours, and I was too tired.

"What are you waiting for?" he asked.

"I have not paid for my beer yet."

"I'll take care of that. Go home and get your things ready!"

I thanked him and stumbled wearily back to the farm. That was one of the most horrible nights I have ever spent.

Each moment I was aware that secret police might rattle the door and get me out of bed to escort me to prison. When the morning finally came I was happy that nothing had happened. I had no choice but to flee to the West. I would have liked very much to stay with those people and continue working there, especially since they had done so much for me. The boss had given me one of his suits and some of his shirts so that I could look at least somewhat like a cultivated person. But my freedom was more. valuable at that point than any obligation. I knew if I stayed I probably would have had to suffer behind barbed wire for another two years.

It just so happened—by coincidence or intervention—that there were two men from the English Zone at that time in the Eastern Zone. I never had talked to anybody who lived in the English Zone, but one of these two men had formerly worked at the farm where I was working. Since they were going back the same day to the English Zone, I decided to accompany them. I did my last business in town and said good-bye to the good people there; I left with my two companions by train, headed toward the Western Zone. We traveled out of our way to the north because they said it was easier to get over the border there.

Late that night the train stopped at a depot and we all got off the train, this time from the passenger car. Grabbing our belongings, we went into the waiting room. The place was crowded already since many people had been held up here because there were no connection. We looked at the timetable and saw that the next train would leave in the morning. We were stranded.

Looking around, we saw that all the tables were occupied. There was no place to sit; we were engulfed by the thick air and cigarette smoke. I was reminded of a similar experience at Insterburg. Suddenly a family got up and left and we were finally seated again. We put our luggage down and tried to sleep on the table, but I was too excited to sleep much. Thoughts of the British Zone filled my mind, but we were still in the Russian Zone. After a while I dozed off a little. My friends had fallen fast asleep and I could hear them snoring. The door was banging; people were milling out and milling in. When I looked up, I saw two German railroad police were entering. My heart started to beat faster. After all, I was a fugitive. They started to check identity cards, beginning at the first table. I knew I could not leave without looking suspicious.

Now they were at the next table. Despite the panic rising within me, I put my head down and acted as if I were sleeping. They were so close that I smelled their new uniforms. Out of the corner of my eye I saw them shake my neighbor. He appeared bewildered, but then he reached for his pocket. I did not dare to look at the policeman but kept my head lowered. I felt my cheeks getting red; I was afraid that I would betray myself. My other friend was being checked.

"Where are you from?" asked the policeman.

"From the British Zone."

"What are you doing here?" The old question was repeated.

"We visited friends and now we are on the way back."

"And who is this man here?" I could feel that he was pointing at me. Then I felt him shaking me. I tried to prolong waking up. But I knew I would have to look at his face and then, I feared, everything would be over. Before I knew it I would be going back to Russia.

There was a shuffling at the door. Another policeman entered the room. My heart sank even further and I gave up hope.

"You're to come and guard a coal train," shouted the newly arrived policeman across the room to the other guard.

I couldn't believe it! The diversion was my reprieve! When both the policemen left the room, I felt as if a burden had been taken off my shoulders. The next morning we boarded another train.

Finally we came to a place where the train stopped. From there we had to leave it behind and walk over to the West.

At that time it was not so hard to cross the border. A few policemen on the Western side of the border checked once in awhile to see whether anybody had alcohol with them, because this was one of the black-market articles which was smuggled over the border quite frequently. Actually it was about three miles to the other side of the border. We had to walk along the railroad tracks which were not used any more between the West and the East. We three fellows took turns helping a lady we had met on the train carry her baggage over to the West Zone.

Shortly before we reached the West Zone we were stopped by two People's Policemen. They accosted us shortly before Helmstedt. One was especially interested in me and asked me where I was going. I told him the truth, that I was going to visit some of my relatives. He checked my passport and told me to open my suitcase. After he had checked my identification, he said what I was afraid I would hear. "We just received a list today. The police of East Germany are looking for you."

I was quite shocked when he told me that. But he continued and I began to understand what it was all about.

"Some of the new clothes you have in your suitcase were stolen in East Germany." He mentioned the name of the county seat and the village where I came from. I was relieved because his information was wrong.

While we were arguing back and forth the other guard pushed him to the side and said with a smile, "The train is already waiting at the station. Let him go!"

It was only about a hundred yards to the West German train depot. I packed my suitcase again and walked over there. The train was waiting, the heated steam engine ready for the trip. We got on the train as the sun was setting in the west. After we had gone a short distance the day came to a close. My mind went back to what the old lady had said when the Russians captured me: "May the Lord bless you, Horst." Then I remembered also what the well-meaning butcher said to me: "We've got to survive."

199

WESTERN ZONE

My crossing of the border into Western Germany was a
farewell to all I had known. I said good-bye to the East. I
said good-bye to another world. I left the Reds. But the
nightmares of the days under their control would never leave
me.

It was a real joy to sit in a train without the feeling of
being constantly followed. My first destination was Hannover, where I had some relatives. Arriving in this demolish-
ed city at midnight, it seemed best to stay in the train depot
until morning.

It was the year 1947 and thousands or even millions of
people were constantly moving about, trying to find their
loved ones fleeing from the East. Others were seeking work,
or being released out of captivity by one of the victorious
nations.

There was a crowd milling around in the depot, but later
I observed that many of them went down to the air-raid
shelter in the cellar. Being accustomed to following the
crowd, I went along with them. Hundreds of people were
already assembled in the basement, lying on the floor, sitting
about, or standing. I was very tired myself and decided to
lie down. I spread out a few belongings and put the rest
under my head. It wasn't safe to leave anything unguarded,
even though a policeman was constantly on watch in the air-
raid shelter.

At about 4 A.M.. I decided to get up and walk toward my
uncle'ş home.

This early morning walk was like walking through the
ruins of Sodom or Gomorrah. Whole houses, city blocks,
streets, even entire sections of the city had been completely
destroyed by Allied planes. Rubbish was lying several yards
high along the sidewalks. Holes in the pavement were filled
with dirt. The ruins of former mansions towered in a ghost-
like appearance. Only the main street and the intersections
were lit up. Otherwise it was dark.

This certainly was not the West I had expected. Instead of flourishing cities, I found rubbish heaps; instead of well-clad people, there were shabby prisoners; instead of friendly people, I encountered insecure strangers. I was discouraged. My despair was so great that I was almost ready to return to my old boss in the East Zone. But I finally reached the home and was shown a bed where I slept until morning.

The joy of my reunion with my relatives was great. The last time our family had been together was in 1944. Since that time we had been scattered from our homes in the East all over Germany, Russia, and Poland. We spent the forenoon exchanging past experiences, and in the afternoon I left by train to go to another uncle's place about twenty-five miles from Hannover. I boarded an overcrowded train and arrived at the railroad depot about 3:00 in the afternoon. I was told that my uncle lived in a former monastery which was now a state-owned farm that had been rented out to a farmer, with about a thousand acres of land.

Uncle Neufeldt had started out in those critical days of January, 1945, with sixteen horses and several wagons loaded with his own family and the families of the people who worked for him. They had barely escaped the Russian spearhead by fleeing over the ice of the Vistula River, since the bridges were overcrowded. After several months of a tiresome journey they arrived at this place in Lower Saxony. On the way two of his employees had complained that their horses couldn't keep up with the rest. So he told them to rest a few days and meet him at another city. These people never appeared and my uncle lost eight horses and two wagons. They had taken him in with a scheme to gain possession of all the horses and wagons. They stopped in the Russian Zone where it was impossible for my uncle to claim his rights.

Living in West Germany I had to make new adjustments. I had to relearn how to eat meat with a knife and fork. I had to learn again how to tip my hat in respect before important people. I had to change some of my expressions, observe courtesy, and do many other things which belong to a civilized and polished society. In the East Zone everything had been conducted on a more common level.

EMPLOYMENT

It had been simple to enter the West Zone by crossing the border as long as my visit was temporary. But to stay longer, and this was what I had in mind, I needed special permission.

In those days West Germany was very crowded with refugees and returning prisoners. Schleswig-Holstein and Lower Saxony were overrun. In front of each village was a sign telling everybody who passed that no one could take up residence there except by permit. In most of the villages the population had doubled since the end of the war. People who had lost their homes in the city during bombing days had moved out into the country; others who had found that the food supply was better in the country than in the city had also moved in. Refugees, displaced persons and many others were constantly coming into the villages. There was certainly no shortage of manpower.

In order to find work for me, my uncle called the employment office and inquired about a job opening. Since I was single it was not quite so hard to find an opening as it would have been for a man with a family, because the larger group would need its own cooking facilities and more space to sleep. There was an opening I took in a neighboring village. We walked over one evening after I had been at my uncle's place about a week and talked matters over with my future boss. Only after I had assured him that I was able to work hard did he accept me. His farm consisted of about forty-five acres of land, some of which was in woods and the rest in tillable land and pasture.

The work was not easy. We had two horses and an ox for plowing and for hauling the wagons, and we had to work constantly in order to keep up and to compete with our neighbors.

One of my cousins had attended the agricultural school during the winter sessions the last two years. My uncle and aunt were interested in my getting more education. They hoped that I might become an administrator and arrive at a more socially acceptable position. In the beginning I was not very anxious to attend school, but finally I consented and attended the session of the winter 1947-48.

This was not easy either since I had to work for my room and board. I got up at 5:30, cleaned the stables of the cows and the horses, and ate breakfast in a hurry. Then I changed clothes, ran to the bus, and arrived at the school by 7:30. The school started at 8:00 and lasted until about 1:00. Usually I returned by bus at 2:00, but sometimes when the school was dismissed at noon I preferred to walk the two miles in order to get home earlier. Then I ate dinner hurriedly and rushed to do my assigned work. In the evening after 7:00 I did assignments and went to bed. My life was ordered like this from November to March.

During the summer I had received from eight to twelve dollars a month. But now during winter, working only half days, I did not receive any money but worked for room and board. Often I had to make up on Sunday what I could not do during the week. But this time also passed by quickly. I passed the farm-laborer test in the spring. Now I had to go to another farm and be there two years as a farm-administrator apprentice. My uncle and I had looked around for a suitable farm and finally found one in another village. In the spring of 1948 I went there.

My new boss employed four people regularly and sometimes had twelve or fourteen women working for him in the afternoon. The farm had about 110 acres of land. There were six horses, one tractor, and twenty-five cows. The boss owned several lots in the forest and raised rye, oats, barley, wheat, potatoes, sugar beets, and truck crops.

In the beginning I was assigned a team of horses, the wildest in the whole barn. One day they ran away with a whole set of harrows, ruining them completely, and came back half lame. I had a terrible time concentrating, a situation probably caused by the preceding undernourishment. I felt very ashamed because of this condition. I often forgot to take the doubletree to the field, lost chains, and even forgot wagons. The boss often became greatly upset with me about this, but I could not help it. He also taught me how to drive a tractor and after several lessons remarked that I would never make a driver. But I kept on trying and finally was able to manage a tractor with at least a certain amount of perfection.

REUNION WITH MOTHER

My mother came over to the West in the spring just at the time when I transferred to this new farm. Obviously I was very happy to see her. But since I had been away from home so long I had lost my sense of affection and could not adequately express my feelings. She was quite disturbed by my undemonstrativeness. My soul still bore scars from the concentration camp. It was inevitable that in confinement and deprivation we had all become egotists. Even family ties and their meaning had been almost completely destroyed from our emotions. Suffering had affected us in mind, body and soul, and we were still far from being the warm human beings of our pre-Russian days.

When I had been at the lowest point of misery in Russia, I had called upon God in my desperation. I had promised the Lord to go into His service if He would be able to deliver me out of that calamity. But the truth is, when I came back I became so entangled in my working permits and difficulties that I forgot all my promises made back there. My main intent now was to try to make the best of my career and climb as quickly as possible into society.

After passing my state examination I was employed on three different farms. My position was that of a working administrator, with the accent on working. It is said that certain people in Europe work to live, but that the Germans live to work. This I found out in more than one way through my different associations.

But how they spent their money was difficult for me to understand. I did not spend my twenty-five-dollar monthly income on drinking, but I had one boss who invested quite a bit of time and money at inns. Drinking was such a common habit in that vicinity that I accepted many drinks in order to make a better impression.

On one farm I received a special privilege from my boss to use one of the riding horses. This was a pleasant diversion. I enjoyed the meetings of the riding club, which I joined. This of course involved practice riding on Sunday. In the short time I was in this club I put in extra practice, especially since the tournament was close at hand. When the tournament came along I was able to win the sixteenth prize in the jumping contest. I was very proud of this accomplishment.

16

RECLAIMED

Since 1944 and my repatriation, I had had no vacation. I really would not have known where or how to spend all the free time. Mother lived in very crowded conditions in a village about fifteen miles away from my working place. I did not want to impose on her. But one Sunday when visiting her for the day, she showed me a letter which invited me to a Christian youth retreat close to the city of Hamburg. Since I didn't have anyplace to go over my vacation, we decided that it would be good for me to go there. The youth retreat was planned for the holiday between Christmas and January 1. The days at the retreat were filled with discussions, lectures and sermons on religion, besides the entertainment and recreation that were featured. I listened with genuine interest. When it was over I realized the retreat had been a wise choice.

I had never been in real Christian company, but I felt that these people had something I did not have. They talked about the meaning of baptism, the need to love one's enemy, and many other things. Although I did not agree with their ideas, the leaders and other members still kept on loving me. The idea of loving one's enemy was completely foreign to me, and I felt that it was a complete impossibility. I had been raised in a nationalistic German atmosphere and had been mistreated by the enemy.

But I also heard there about an international farm-trainee program in America. I had always been interested in America, especially after my return from Russia when I had tried to emigrate there. But the waiting list for emigration was so long then that there was not much hope of leaving for the next five or six years. But now I saw another chance that could bring me to this land of promise. To tell the truth, I was not as much interested in seeing the Christians in America—as the youth retreat leaders thought—as I was in seeing America.

Trip to America

Without too much trouble, after these youth meetings the arrangements were made for me to leave. I would travel by boat in October of 1951. I was excited, and impatient to get underway.

The trip over on the boat was the beginning of many new experiences. There were people of many nations traveling with me. Sometimes there were a Dutchman, a Belgian, even a Russian and a German at the same table. The dominant languages spoken were English and German, but Dutch, French, and Russian could also be heard. I had a good chance to make use of the few Russian terms that I still remembered from my captivity. But I also caught myself frequently speaking English to a Russian and thinking I was speaking Russian, and vice versa. In spite of such difficulties it was surprising how well we got along; everybody made a supreme effort to be congenial.

My final destination was Huron, South Dakota. When I arrived I was greeted at the station by my new boss, his wife, and their little son, who were all eager to see their visitor from Germany. Their grandparents had been German-speaking Christians in Russia. I was very much surprised to hear these folks talk German; but I was also very glad because this made it easy for me to carry on a conversation with them.

LIFE WITH CHRISTIANS

But the attitude which impressed me the most was the piety expressed in the life-style of the people in this area. Instead of cursing when something went wrong, they prayed; instead of complaining over hardships, they offered thanks; instead of listening to jazz, they sang praises to God; instead of idleness, they worked.

Now I began to understand why the Puritans and the Pilgrims, the Brethren, the Methodists, and the Anabaptists had come to this country. It was because they could worship here and practice their deep-seated convictions in a way they wanted without interference.

While at home, hanging over my bed was a picture of a battle in which my grandfather had participated. In my room here there hung a motto saying, "God Is Love." While at home I had had a wild-west book on my desk, here I found a Bible. At home I had looked into the face of the revered Field Marshal von Hindenburg on the walls; here I looked into a picture which bore the likeness of the crucified Lord. At home we had often talked about the ancient hero Leonidas; here we often talked about the living God. Instead of beer, my new friends drank Kool-aid. What a reception for someone who had come just to enjoy America! A whole new set of values was introduced to me.

Before breakfast my hosts held a morning worship service. They went to church twice on Sunday and often attended a midweek prayer meeting, or special Bible conferences. Of course they took me along to most of these meetings, and I had to confess that I attended more church in six weeks there than I had in all my life before. I was impressed by the Sunday school and enjoyed taking part in the discussion. The mission conferences and special Bible conferences were also of great interest to me.

People there often asked me whether or not I was a Christian. I particularly remember one evening when one of the older ministers came and asked me in high German: *"Bist Du ein Christ?"* (Are you a Christian?).

I replied, "Yes, of course."

Then he asked me how I knew that I was one, and I told him that my father had been a Christian. This was all I knew about Christianity at that time. Of course he tried to show me that this relationship was not sufficient. Nevertheless, I thought I was right and wondered why be bothered to question me.

Time went on and I continued to work on the farm and attend church. I remember one Wednesday evening when we had a prayer meeting in the church. The men sat on one side and the women on the other. The minister asked us all to kneel down and then to pray audibly, telling the Lord what was on our hearts. Everybody took his turn and finally mine came. I started to pray, but I really could not. I started shaking like a leaf in the fall wind and uttered something unintelligible. It was the first time that I had been asked to pray in public. I believe now that this was the beginning of my conviction about my hypocrisy toward God. There was good reason why I could not pray; I had never experienced Christ myself and was a skeptic. Returning home with my boss after the meeting, I tried to drown my convictions by talking about anything else but the need of my soul. We talked about the presidential election and politics, for these matters were always closer to my heart than subjects concerning God.

Move to Indiana

After a very enjoyable time in South Dakota, for the second part of my year in the US I went to a farm in Indiana, arriving at my new place near Goshen, Indiana, on May 4,

1952. My new boss lived about three miles from New Paris, Indiana. The farming there was somewhat different since he had more milk cows and lots of poultry. He had about 6,000 broad-breasted turkeys and 6,000 white chickens besides sixteen purebred cows. Taking care of these and the land which was under cultivation gave us plenty to do.

My boss, and perhaps other people there, must have sensed my unconverted state right from the beginning. I remember especially one day when they took me along to a revival meeting which was conducted by Hyman Appelman, a converted Jew, in a large building in South Bend. When this man preached and shared his concern about the need of his own people, the Jews, I also felt a compassionate need for my people in Germany. Nevertheless, I did not feel a personal need. When he was preaching and denouncing the sinner, I still felt that I was good enough and that he was not talking to me. Certainly he was talking rather to all drunkards, smokers, adulterers, and other sinners on the right and left side of myself. *Am I a sinner too?* I wondered. *Of course not,* I rationalized. *I don't do a lot of those things anyway. I don't smoke, I don't drink, and I'm living what one would call a good moral life.*

My boss, Maynard Hoover, was very enthusiastic one day when he heard that another evangelistic campaign would be conducted in the Goshen area. At the end of August the Brunk Brothers Evangelistic Campaign came to that section and pitched their large six-pole tent about two miles from Goshen. When we went to these meetings it seemed as if the Spirit of God was moving among the people. But I still believed that this emphasis was directed to turn the really "great" sinners from their evil ways. I did not feel much need for myself.

COMMITMENT

The third night George Brunk preached on the power of the early church, about how the people received the Holy

211

Ghost, and how they went about praising God and making disciples. This early church described in the book of Acts grew daily. I again thought about my people back in Germany and wondered why we could not have had experiences such as this and why I could not help my own people. But during this message I suddenly awoke to the realization that I could not do this without making a commitment myself before God. The Spirit of God convinced me that I first had to get right with God myself before I would be able to help someone else.

I came under tremendous conviction. Many of the events of my life passed through my mind. The proud German, the stiff nationalist, the hater of the Jews, the secret sinner, the militarist, the enemy of the Russians—all these images of myself were running in vain competition for superiority in my life. And I was wondering if they should be taken out of their doubtful existence and be replaced by something better.

"And the Spirit and the bride say, Come. And let him that heareth say, Come. And let him that is athirst come. And whosoever will, let him take the water of life freely." These words from the Bible in Revelation 22:17 intrigued me.

Was this water of life also for me? Was that blood also shed for me? Finally I responded to the invitation. I started to walk to the altar and heard a voice behind me saying: "God bless you!" I went forward and received Christ as my personal Savior in the prayer room. It was the finale of the first part of my life; the life of an unconverted man was finished and the life of the new man started. I, Horst Gerlach, had met the God who had spared me for just this hour.

From this day on things have been different for me. Whereas I used to look at life from a purely human and egotistical point of view, I now see it in the Christian perspective. I received a completely new understanding of the claims of Christ upon His people and now have laid aside my earlier attitudes through His grace.

I felt a new attitude toward my fellowmen, regardless of nationality or color. And now I realized that the things which I had thought were of extreme value, like nationalism and militarism, were as nothing compared to eternal life in the kingdom of Christ. It was really true for me—old things had passed away; all things had become new. Now I knew what John meant when he said, "We know that we have passed from death unto life, because we love the brethren."

It was a change for me in countless ways: from an unforgiven sinner to a forgiven sinner, from hypocrisy to open confession, from hate to love, from evil to good, and from darkness to light.

Now the interventions of my earlier life took on greater meaning. The lessons I had learned in my suffering were not unknown to God. He alone had spared my life for the greater glory of His name.

EPILOGUE

I was born on February 5, 1929, in a little village called *Neuendorf-Hoehe* in East Prussia. Our county seat was Elbing. Our village was an average village with about 260 inhabitants, most of whom were either farmers or farm employees. Some went away to work in the city, but this was the exception and was not liked much by the other villagers.

My father was a fairly successful farmer with about 200 acres of land. The main crops were rye, wheat, oats, flax, barley, potatoes and, in the later years, sugar beets. We had about twenty-five Holstein-Friesian cows. Land work was done with fourteen to sixteen horses. About six families worked regularly for us in the fields and my mother usually had two or three girls helping in the kitchen.

I grew up in a time when the political unrest following the First World War had begun to settle. The worldwide depression was disappearing and the new national "messiah" of the German people, Adolf Hitler, had arisen. Many splinter parties and various philosophies were united into one party and one common effort: "to regain for Germany the place in the family of nations that it once held." Hitler had worked himself up from the office of corporal in the World War I imperial army to the powerful position of Chancellor of the Third Reich. He seized power on January 30, 1933. His opposition on the left, represented by communism and socialism, and his opposition on the right, represented by nationalism and capitalism, had been either wiped out or absorbed by the National Socialistic German Labor Party (NSDAP). Everybody seemed well pleased. There was work and there was money. There seemed to be general prosperity.

At the age of six, I started to attend our small grade school in the village. The teacher was typical in that he had a cow, a few acres of land, and several dozen hives of bees to supplement his salary.

Our grades were all in one room. Since I was the son of one of the biggest farmers in the village, I was supposed to be smarter than the rest of the others. However, this was not always true. For during my second year, I completely flunked a test. The teacher told me to stretch out my hands, and I received two stripes in each with a stick, according to the old-fashioned way.

Since my early boyhood I was interested in history and politics, listening to the newscasts and reading the headlines of the newspapers while others were playing outside. Not that I never played with them, but I was much more interested in the romance of human events.

LUTHERAN—MENNONITE HERITAGE

My father was, as far as his relation to God was concerned, a Christian of the Lutheran faith. My mother had been a Mennonite, coming from the Danzig-West Prussian area. My father's forefathers were probably Lutherans who were ex-

pelled from Salzburg and settled in East Prussia by King
Frederick William I (1713-40) of Prussia. The area had been
depopulated by the plague and was resettled by persecuted
Lutherans.

With the beginning of my conscious thinking and communication came also the thought of God. It is not hard for
a child to recognize that there is a supernatural Being who
executes His wrath upon the disobedient and bestows His
love upon those who fear Him and keep His commandments.
Thus I thought God was a great man who had the stature of
a grandfather with a great white beard and dark piercing
eyes. Especially during thunderstorms and during the night
I felt God's threatening presence.

Mother taught us boys formal prayers to use when we went
to bed, but we never prayed at the table. When we were invited to the pastor's home I observed that one member of
his family led in prayer before the meal. This and other in-
cidents caused me to conclude that intercession was the job
of the clergy and that the average member did not need to
worry much about it. But when my grandmother died in
1937 and I saw a Bible which had been placed by her head,
I almost trembled at the sight of it, thinking this must be a
holy book, perhaps a book which deals with the dead; could
it also be a book for the living?

The ax, the Bible, and the sword were the main in-
struments used in settling the regions of eastern Germany.
By the time I was growing up, the ax of the frontiersman had
been replaced by modern implements, and the Bible was
slowly being replaced by Hitler's new bible, *Mein Kampf*
("My Struggle"). Meanwhile, only the sword remained to
dominate, to oppress, and to annex by force if necessary.

Under Hitler, Germany became highly organized, specialized, and centralized. There was the general Nazi party

whose members met several times during the month to have political talks and instructions. There was the SA (storm troopers), a para-military organization (similar to the American National Guard) which often practiced marching and drilling with guns, and greatly emphasized sports. All members wore uniforms and mostly younger men joined. The SS (*Schutz-Staffel* or "protection force") had developed with the SA from the times when a special guard was needed to protect Hitler and his meetings before he was in office. After Hitler seized power, this movement grew into one of his strongest political supports, being composed of the most devout and dedicated Nazis. There was the NSKK, a motorized SA. They practiced, especially on Sunday, with motorcycles, trucks, and cars in driving, going up the hills and through the ditches in order to prepare the drivers for a future assignment with the army in driving tanks or trucks through the country without using roads.

The most interesting creation of that time was the German Working Front. Hitler and his associates had succeeded in getting labor and management under one common administration. This organization was, of course, also sponsored by the Nazi party and served as mediator between labor and management, abolishing strikes and walkouts. It also sponsored trips and fairs. A whole fleet of boats was built in order to take the workers during vacation time out into the Baltic, North or Mediteranean seas. These ships were built to be used later as troop-transport ships. They were called KDF boats, which translated meant "power through joy."

WHY WAS HITLER POPULAR?

The reason why Germans followed Hitler was both simple and complex. In 1918 Germany had lost the First World War, a loss which set off a whole series of chain reactions. After the treaty of Versailles, Germany lost considerable land, as well as her colonies, and had to pay $33 million to the victorious nations. The navy was sunk by her crew while they were delivering it to England for reparation. The French established bridgeheads at Cologne, Trier and Coblenz. The once-proud imperial army was reduced to 100,000 men, and there was general economic depression. There was a communist revolution; the emperor had to go, and things went from bad to worse.

Later the nation recovered slightly, but the constant reparations to the victorious nations caused inflation. In one year all the money became worthless. In the end, a million marks were needed in order to buy a box of matches. Older people, who all their lives had saved money, lost it overnight, becoming completely helpless in their old age. Many farmers lost their farms because they were unable to pay their debts and taxes. Laborers received low wages and unemployment was high (at one time reaching six million). Ten cents was an average hourly wage. Sometimes up to 120 different political parties were following leaders who thought they knew the solution to Germany's ills.

The whole world was in a state of depression. Wages could not be paid, workers could not be hired, and products could not be sold for a favorable price. During that time there was always the popular cry in Germany for a "strong man." In 1925 Field Marshal von Hindenburg, one of the most distinguished German heroes of World War I, was elected president. But since he was quite old and no longer energetic, he somewhat discouraged the conservative people who had elected him.

During all this time, another man was struggling for power. He started out as a public speaker and joined a small rightist party in 1919. Then he became one of their main leaders, and the party soon grew much larger. In 1923, during a protest demonstration designed to overthrow the Bavarian government, the police opened fire into his marching columns, killing sixteen, wounding others. He himself was captured and brought to a fortress. Here he wrote a book called *Mein Kampf*. When he was released, he started to rebuild his party, finally gaining power on January 30, 1933, having received 230 votes out of 500 during the election of the Reichstag, the lower house of Parliament.

President Hindenburg died in 1934. Hitler proclaimed that no one was worthy to take the president's position. Thus he had all the power of president and chancellor in his hands, especially after a law was passed giving him complete liberty.

With the seizure of power, all parliamentary procedure ceased except the Reichstag, which was made up of appointed party officials. Some called it the best-paid male chorus in the world, for its main function was to applaud Hitler's speeches and acts and to sing the national anthem and the *Horst Wessel* song after the Führer's addresses.

The papers talked much about the simplicity of the new chancellor who neither smoked nor drank, nor had time to get married since he was so occupied with the "welfare" of the German people.

WORK AND BREAD

Most important, Hitler was able to secure work and bread for the people. Even though their freedom had to be sacrificed, their primary interest was taken care of. A German proverb says: "Love comes through the stomach." In other words, if someone knows how to feed his people, he'll be loved by them.

Hitler was so popular because the people had found new security. Everybody was employed and received a fairly good wage. The farmers were promised guaranteed prices, enabling them again to calculate and think ahead. The young men could receive social recognition by joining the army, and the rearming of the whole nation brought employment for factory workers and fast advancement for the more ingenious.

Couples who had many children received government aid, and school tuition was paid. Medals were given to women who had many children. Naturally this was done to increase the birthrate and to supply the nation with new blood for a future war.

Through the re-creation of a new army, the nation's national spirit was satisfied. Old soldiers and nationalists found satisfaction in this new national sport. The occupation of Austria, of former German territories, and of other parts of Europe containing German ethnic groups augmented the well-being of all zealous nationalists. Former skeptics of Hitler became satisfied and blinded by the obvious successes. Thus many deep thinkers and even those with much experience were caught off guard.

Nevertheless, some foresaw the outcome of all this. There were people who were loyal to their divine Master, Jesus, and refused to sanction the Jewish persecutions. There were honest politicians who were opposed to Hitler's political views, including some Conservatives, Social Democrats, and others. Many of them were jailed or put in concentration camps. Quite a few old soldiers remembered the outcome of World War I and therefore opposed this new militarism. But this was not true of the mass of the people, so Hitler's opponents were overwhelmed in the turmoil of public opinion.

Thus it went on. The great Autobahn (turnpike) system was built. The Volkswagen (People's Car) was to be made available at a low price. Many political gatherings were arranged; nationalism was intensified. In his speeches, Hitler emphasized that he was a peace-loving man. But speaking about a peaceful world is not the same as creating one.

INFLUENCE ON YOUTH

In 1939 I began attending high school in our county seat.

221

Much emphasis was placed on the subjects of German, arithmetic, English, and Latin. But sports were stressed most. It was very hard to be promoted to another class if one failed in sports. At the beginning we received about one hour a week of religious instruction, but this ceased at the onset of the war when our religious teacher was drafted into the army.

Our faith in God was constantly undermined in our natural science classes. Our biology teacher told us that he who believes in God and does not believe in evolution makes a fool of himself.

At the age of ten, I joined the *Jungvolk* (Young Folk), as required by law. Every healthy German boy or girl had to join either the Young Folk or Young Women's Club, the junior organizations of the Hitler Jugend (Hitler Youth). Exercises were held twice a week for two hours.

Universally, it seems, a youngster is pressured to conform to his society and especially to his age group. When we saw the older boys doing their exercises in the Hitler Youth, we were attracted, especially since they wore uniforms.

The Hitler Youth was divided into many specialized sections. Most were in the general Hitler Youth, but others were in the motorized division, practicing with motorcycles; in the flying section, building model planes and flying real planes; in the radio group, practicing with radios, or in the marine division whose main emphasis was training in steering a sailboat, in swimming, in signaling, and other fundamentals of the navy.

The Hitler Youth had been organized with one main purpose—to prepare the youth for the later military service. To accomplish this goal, we played warlike games outdoors, although we did not use weapons. We practiced camouflaging, crawling on the ground with the least visibility, carrying dispatches, patrolling, and other army skills.

We also practiced marching, including goose-stepping. We sang patriotic songs, especially those which dealt with

222

war, victory, and "heroic" death for the fatherland. On rainy or on snowy days we received political instructions, discussing our nation, contemporary affairs, and the history of the Nazi party. We were all drilled in self-discipline and strict obedience to our superiors.

We also were hardened against the climate. We ran around in shorts, slept out in tents, and spent lots of time outdoors to become used to the climate. We were conditioned for physical endurance through exercises such as athletic games, long marches, and long bicycle tours. Each year we had a sports festival at which the winners received awards. The whole nation was converted into an army camp; without any special announcement, we had universal military training.

The leader of our company was the son of our Lutheran pastor. This young man was quite intelligent and also ruthless. During the war he was drafted, and afterward was made a high school principal under the Communist system. Thus he changed from Christianity to fanatic Nazism and from there to fanatic Communism. He even wrote to my mother in the West Zone in 1952, trying to persuade her to adopt his Communistic ideals.

The Hitler Youth meetings were often planned for Sunday forenoon, so that it was impossible for us to attend church. I was in church only a few times during the war. Nevertheless, when I became fourteen, I wanted to be confirmed as my brothers and my other relatives had been. I had missed the general instruction meetings which usually last for two years, but I learned that I could be confirmed if I would attend the instruction meetings for about three months. Thus I was confirmed in 1943. This day was one of the last times that I attended church during the war. Although we were not forbidden to go to church, the general attitude was not favorable toward church attendance.

Many devices were employed to keep the German youth from having a concept of loyalty to a heavenly Father but, on the contrary, to develop the deepest loyalty to the fatherland. Youth consecrations were designed to substitute for conformation. Many thought this was the real thing. "Is not death a long way off? Religion is for the older people; why bother with it when one is young? Is not all our life before us, and does not our *Führer* Hitler get along without God?"

Once or twice a year we had camps, especially over Pentecost or during the Easter or summer vacation. There we had stepped-up training. We became used to sleeping in straw sheds or outdoors, whether it was raining, snowing, or the sun was shining. We became accustomed to being away from home. Our company of about 120 boys was recruited from over ten villages.

Once in a while we did something constructive, like helping with the harvest during the wartime, collecting tea for the drugstores, and building toys for the children during the time when the factories could not make these things, being occupied with war production.

After I had been in the Hitler Youth for about two years, I became tired of the outfit, especially because I was busy with schoolwork. So I dropped out for about six months till a superior came to remind me that everybody had to attend the meetings. So I joined again after receiving a promise of promotion. Later I gave political or historical instructions in our company. Still later I became an adjutant and finally, about three days before the Russians entered our home, I was promoted to be leader of a company.

FATHER'S ARMY EXPERIENCE

During World War I, my father had been an army lieutenant, leading a supply column for the artillery. For several years he also had been an economic administrator in Poland. Although he already was of considerable age when Hitler took over, he was drafted twice between 1933 and 1939. During this time he was trained and brought militarily up to date, promoted to first lieutenant, and later to captain. Shortly before the war started, he had been drafted and put in charge of a supply company in the staff of the Twenty-first Infantry Division. So he was in the army when the war began in the summer of 1939.

I well remember when the war began. We were awakened before dawn by a constant humming of airplane motors. We went to the window to look out, but although the planes seemed to be flying very low, it was too cloudy to see them. About seven o'clock Mother came and told us four boys that she had just heard over the radio that war had broken out. We were quite astonished, and did not know whether to rejoice or feel sorry. After all, we were only sixty miles from the border. Besides that, Father was in the army.

We had not been waiting for a war. Nevertheless, we probably favored the idea once war was declared, since we had great confidence in our government and strong army.

At ten o'clock Hitler spoke to the Reichstag. All of us were eager to hear his speech. I don't remember much anymore, but I do know that he said, "My patience is over; since 5:11 o'clock in the morning, our troops are shooting back."

> Over a period of four months, I have been looking on. . . . I proposed a solution on the basis of direct negotiation. For two long days, I have been waiting. . . .My love of peace and my endless patience should not be mistaken for weakness. I am now determined to talk the same language to Poland that Poland has been talking to us. I have given in to the Western powers for quite some time. . . .I myself am today and will be from now on, nothing but the soldier of the German *Wehrmacht;* just as I fought in the last war, so will I fight now. I shall not take off this uniform until we have achieved victory. . . .However, if something should happen to me, I want the German people to know that I have appointed Hermann Goering to become my successor. If something should happen to him, my deputy, Rudolph Hess, will take his place; and if something should happen to Hess, the Senate which I

will soon appoint will elect his successor; the man must be worthy to succeed me—that is to say, the bravest man. I never knew what the word capitulation means!*

Thus the greatest war this earth has ever witnessed had started.

This speech sounds rather ridiculous today, but at the time it was made, many Germans could not see that it was an attempted self-justification and that Germany would be forced later to an unconditional surrender.

Since there was a manpower shortage, all of us boys had to help in the potato harvest. From there we could hear the thunder of the battle in Poland and were told later the battleship *Schleswig-Holstein* was pounding Polish fortifications in the Danzig area. Most of Poland was occupied during an eighteen-day period, with the exception of Warsaw and a few other strongholds. Afterward we saw the victorious soldiers coming home, having defeated that brave little country.

Polish civilian prisoners were brought to Germany and some were assigned to work for us. The Nazi government said they were to be treated as enemies since the Poles had mistreated quite a few ethnic Germans. However, when I saw these people, I could not hate them since they looked completely innocent. But the nationalistic spirit soon overtook all the Germans. What could not be done by propaganda and mass education was done by public pressure.

NATIONALISM

Even traditional believers in nonresistant love for enemies, such as the Mennonites had been, were carried away by the spirit of nationalism. Many of my Mennonite cousins and friends were in the army and public offices, advancing just as fast as all the rest of the Germans. Even

---

* *Time* magazine (Sept. 4, 1939).

though some of the ministers had been in favor of nonresistance, the young people in cooperation with the SS had pressured the preachers so long that they had finally yielded. Since economic problems had been solved by the introduction of guaranteed prices for grain, livestock, poultry, and dairy products, these Mennonite farmers had overlooked what was behind the scene.

The fact that scattered settlements in Poland, Danzig and East Germany were united into one common fatherland after the beginning of the war in 1939, added to their national spirit. When they discovered that militant Nazism was at the same time engaged in a struggle against the Jews and the confessing church of Jesus Christ, and the world at large, it was too late for a return to sound Christianity.

In 1940 my father was transferred to the western front with the army that was to conquer France. Mother had quite a job in managing all the farm work, since the labor situation was complicated and she did not always receive the best cooperation from us boys and from our employees. Nevertheless, she managed to get along all right with some good advice from Father by mail and from our neighbors.

The war went on. Denmark and Norway were invaded on April 9, 1940; France, Holland, Belgium, and Luxembourg, on May 10. Even though Father was not very close to the front lines, we had to reckon with the fact that he was in danger.

In the beginning we were quite shocked that our army went through Holland, Belgium, and Luxembourg in order to conquer France. But the later explanation that this was a "military necessity" satisfied most of us.

We all marveled over the army's success and were especially attracted by the new arms and war methods. We heard with wonder of the parachute troops who contributed much to the success of the battles in the West. The eyes of the nation were also attracted by the tremendous advances of the armored forces under the leadership of General

227

Guderian. Father's division went as far as Lyon in southern France. Later on, parts of the army were moved back to Germany and his division entered our city with a glamorous parade. We boys were especially proud since we knew Father was on the staff of that division and had received another medal besides the Iron Cross of World War I. The staff was placed in our high school building so we were forced to have school in the afternoon one week and the next week in the forenoon. When our school became an army hospital, we moved out completely and shared the girls' school.

In 1939 most Germans could not understand why Hitler made a pact with Soviet Russia, since the two philosophies of communism and Nazism had been quite opposed. Although both were totalitarian dictatorships and had certain methods in common, their general views and ideologies were opposite. While the philosophy of communism is government ownership and control, Fascism is more or less a mixed form of controlled private capitalism and socialism. The second main difference lies in the racial ideology as represented by the Nazis.

But this peaceful coexistence with Russia did not last. Germany received wheat and other agricultural products, plus oil, from Russia, and exchanged, almost to the last, weapons and ammunition that were not standardized enough for the German army.

My uncle told me later that the German army had given a contract to various firms that would produce the best anti-aircraft gun of a middle-heavy caliber. One factory had mistakenly produced over a thousand wrong-sized guns. Since the whole army was supposed to have standardized material, the guns were sold to the Russians. During the Russian occupation, German soldiers found that they had been fired on by German guns.

Since 1939 Russia had occupied parts of Poland and also Latvia, Lithuania, and Estonia, and now had a long border line with Germany. The two buffer states, Lithuania and Poland, had been eradicated, and Germany felt herself quite open from the East, to be occupied any moment by the Russians. So in not much longer than several weeks, the whole invasion army was shifted from the western front to the eastern front.

WAR BEGINS

We lived close to the main railroad toward the East, where we sometimes saw 100 or 130 trains a day rolling east loaded with troops. Tanks, guns, soldiers, horses, and surplus material were shipped. Finally, without any warning, the German guns opened fire on the morning of June 22. Some said that even to the hour before the invasion, trains with grain or with other products had gone from the East to the West, but all this ended in the most serious phase of World War II.

My father was with the invading army. His division was in the northern part of the front, advancing toward Leningrad. He again had his old job, but he did not enjoy it much. Now that he was sixty years old, he was physically unable to bear the strains of a modern military campaign. But he was still required to endure the pace of younger soldiers.

Since the losses during the occupation of Poland and the Western countries had not been too high, not many soldiers' obituaries were published in the papers. But this changed when the war with Russia started. The victory which the German army won there had to be bought with extremely heavy losses. At least fifteen to twenty obituaries appeared each day in the county newspaper. At least twelve were killed in action from our village of about 260 inhabitants. Many more were displaced later and died in Russia. At the end of the war there was practically no family that had not lost at least one loved one. Many had lost two, three, four, or even five and more.

229

At the beginning of the war, one regiment of SS troops was in battle. Later they were multiplied to several army corps. Men in these troops were all tall, selected for their physical stamina and political fanaticism. They received special training and special weapons, and were usually sent where the fighting was hottest. Since they were a top unit and especially indoctrinated with Nazism, they were intensely hated by the Russians. If the Russians captured one of them, they executed him immediately, and the SS reacted similarly. Thus there was constant retaliation between these two groups when they met on the front lines.

One of our former Hitler Youth leaders had joined the SS troops and was with a heavy-tank regiment. During one engagement with the Russians, one tank was rendered unmovable and its crew taken prisoner by the Russians. During a counterattack, the other SS men found their comrades shot to death with their tongues cut out. The next time the SS caught some prisoners they retaliated by tying them to the exhaust pipes of their tanks and driving toward the Russian trenches. When the exhaust pipes became hot, the prisoners burned to death while the tanks were driven up and down along the front lines.

What were a few men to the war machine in those days? There were "high ideals" to be defended. Thus the fierceness of the fighting became worse and worse the farther the war progressed. Both armies were wounding and robbing, crushing and burning, shooting and killing, making a chain reaction with no mercy, no end in sight.

The eastern campaign started after Hitler's own formula, without warning, as in a so-called *Blitz* (flash). The German air force was able to knock out most of the Russian air bases and the German army was able to occupy large territory. In a short time about three and a half million Russians were taken prisoner.

Including some other smaller nations, Germany occupied a territory approximately as vast as Germany, England and

France combined. About 132 divisions marched into Russia; a gigantic battle resulted, and Moscow was almost taken. We boys sat at home and were sorry that we were not big enough to be among the soldiers. We had heard about some of the horrors of war, but we had been brought up in such a patriotic spirit that we were anxious to help in spite of that. We also coveted the Iron Crosses and other medals given to brave soldiers. I looked at each passing soldier to determine his bravery by the number of medals he had, anxious to outdo all of them if I would only have a chance.

But I also experienced a tremendous internal conflict. On the one hand we were taught by our parents not to shoot, or even aim at, any man, and on the other hand the state expected us to be ready to kill our enemies anytime. On the one hand there was my faint knowledge of Christ as the Prince of Peace, who said, "Love your enemies. . .do good to them that hate you," and on the other hand there was the state who said, "Those enemies are members of an inferior race; kill to survive."

Why Did Germany Lose?

Scholars disagree somewhat over the question: Why did Germany lose the war? Geographical, political, economic or military reasons are given. When I was only nine years old my grade school teacher told us that we would always have trouble with our neighbors, since we lived in a land surrounded by other nations, with few well-defined geographical borders such as exist in England, and no well-defined ethnic settlements such as exist in Spain. Thus we could always have to expect hostile neighbors and, in case they become too plentiful, war and defeat would be our fate. This opinion parallels that of the political reasoners who say that the Nazi government could not procure enough allies, and thus had to lose.

Others say that the Reich and her allies were economically and militarily exhausted and thus the final defeat had to

231

come. However, now that I have become a Christian, I see things differently. In the first place, war would not have had to come if the nation had lived a Christlike life in peace and harmony with fellow countrymen and foreigners. Second, divine wrath had to come upon this nation and will come over any nation which forgets God and worships idols.

Another cause of the spiritual breakdown of the German nation was the anti-Semitism, sown for many decades in the German mind and finally coming to a culmination in Himmler, chief of the Gestapo; Rosenberg, philosopher of the party; and Hitler, chief of them all. Alfred Rosenberg in his book, *Mythos of the 20th Century,* supplied the confused fancies for the new Nordic religion, with the sun as its symbol. A few Christians, the so-called "Confessing Church," opposed these ideas, but the rest of the church yielded, forming the so-called "German Christians" who fought against Christian world citizenship and tried to get the "Jewish" component out of the Christian doctrine. All I remember concerning this from my earliest youth was the fact that our Jewish friends and businessmen did not appear anymore and, later on in our catecism instruction meetings, our pastor spoke briefly of the Old Testament as some Jewish legend. The aim of these people was the indoctrination, especially of the youth, with the view that they were members of the superior race.

My father had to get busy and obtain the necessary information for his family tree by writing to churches and registration bureaus. Woe unto him who had a close Jewish ancestor! When I look at these race ideas today, and when I am often complimented for belonging to a nation which has produced such great statesmen, poets, musicians, technicians, and even theologians, I often wonder about the progress we have made since those days of race fanaticism.

The atrocities committed in the Buchenwald concentration camp have no equal in history, and the treatment of the

Russian prisoners lacked all marks of humanity, to say nothing of Christianity.

Near the station where we waited for our school bus, there was a newly erected prison camp occupied by Russian prisoners who had helped to finish the Autobahn (turnpike) close to our neighboring village. Sometimes we saw them walk out in the morning for their work assignment and come back in the evening. Often they carried some of their dead fellow prisoners on their shoulders, and about a mile away from the prison camp there was a graveyard where many of these Russians were buried. The reason for their early death was obvious—insufficient food, cruel treatment, and probably little medicine for their sickness. There was quite a contrast between the treatment of Russian prisoners and English prisoners. The English were all well clothed and fed because England and Germany were members of the International Red Cross and prisoners on both sides received Red Cross distributions via Switzerland.

Hitler and other race fanatics had proclaimed that the Russians were inferior human beings and so they were treated inhumanely. This was one of the reasons why Germany lost the war. For, in the beginning, many of the Russian soldiers had given up fighting since they wanted to be loose from the Communistic domination and wanted to help to rebuild their country. But when they found out from escaped prisoners how they were treated, they chose to fight to the end, rather than to be taken into German captivity.

CHRISTIAN OPPOSITION

It is a world-known fact that the Nazis were antagonistic to the church. Although Hitler, Catholic by birth, supposedly paid his church tax to the last day of the war, he did little to help the church. But since Christianity produced a people who loved each other and would even sacrifice their lives in order that others might be saved, and since

Christians always saw a higher obligation toward the heavenly Father than to their civil government, true Christianity and Nazism did not mix.

"Confessing Christians" who opposed the integration of the church program into the state were only a minority. Persecution was not the only method used to make the church submissive. Other means were even more successful. One was the method of substitution. After the Nazis had proclaimed Germans as the superior race, they also found a good substitute for the Christian festivals, reintroducing the old festivals of the Norsemen or of the Germanic tribes. One was the Yule Festival, celebrated by the old Norsemen around Christmastime, on December 22, the winter solstice, at which time the sun reaches its lowest point of the year.

The Norsemen used to get together on this day and celebrate with much beer and fighting. After the Nazi takeover, some of the old Germanic stories were read over the radio during the Christmas season, and we in the Hitler Youth used the material of those stories for our Christmas celebrations. Of course there was a transition period; in the beginning there was only a combination of Christianity and Norse mythology; later on the aim was toward a complete eradication of the Christian Christmas and the substitution of the Norse Yule Festival.

The second Norse festival introduced was the summer solstice, June 21, also called the Sun Festival. The sun is an object which has been revered by many different religions besides the Norsemen. At noon on June 21, the sun reaches its highest point of the whole year. We often celebrated this festival in school or later in the evening with our Hitler Youth company. Marching toward a hill, we piled up wood and brush which was later set afire. Then everyone gathered around and sang praises to the sun. We brought along drums and trumpets to provide special music. Fires could be seen on mountains for miles around. It was as if the whole nation were returning to paganism.

The atheism of German science, the liberalism of German theology, and the Aryan race-ideology had reached its culmination in the Third Reich. Scientists thought they could get along without God, the church thought that the authority of the Bible could only be recognized if it agreed with reason, and the race fanatics thought that their heredity would guarantee them a glorious future forever. In the homes, schools, and public places there hung pictures of Adolf Hitler.

Each morning before school began, one of us boys had the invocation by reciting a quotation from Hitler. I still remember the one I once memorized: "Not men lukewarm and neutralists make history, but those who take war upon themselves!" After that we sang a patriotic song. We also had to memorize the life story of Hitler, with special emphasis on the fact that he was a writer, artist, field commander, and statesman all in one person.

Meanwhile, the Pearl Harbor tragedy had transpired, taking most Germans by surprise. Many of the younger Germans rejoiced, but the older people, still remembering that the entrance of America into World War I had changed the picture completely in favor of the Allies, were not very enthusiastic.

Several days later (Dec. 11, 1941) Hitler declared war on America. Most of us knew that no successful war could be conducted against America, although in the beginning most of the Germans were blinded by the fact that the submarines had so much success along the coast of America. But although they sank about twenty million tons of Allied ships during the whole war, eventually radar caught up with them and made U-boat warfare almost impossible. The German air force and navy tried to raid convoys en route to Russia; sometimes they were successful; more often they were frustrated.

But since war was declared and going strong, everyone tried to do his best to win. We boys received instructions in school that we should help as much as possible with the collection of old metal, paper, bones which would be used to make soap, and old clothing for the production of new. With the further advance of the Allies, Germany and her occupied countries had become what was called "Fortress Europe." Many people still believed in the "wonder weapons" promised by the propaganda ministry and also in the myth that a united Germany could never be defeated.

UNINFORMED CITIZENS

The destructive work done by the police and the SS in concentration camps within Europe was not generally known to the public. Those who knew did not talk, either bound to secrecy by oath or out of fear lest they be taken there for giving away secrets. Thus one was informed about these atrocities only through rumor or personal contacts. Our family first learned of the matter at about the middle of the war when we received a Polish family who were supposed to work for us. The father and his two boys worked very faithfully. Watching this man, one could sense that he was never quite sure whether there was not someone standing behind him.

One Sunday a car came into our yard. Two young men in civilian clothes stepped out and went over to talk to my father. After they had asked him something, my father called me over and told me that I should lead these two men to the place where this Polish man lived. Before we went, one of them went back, got something out of the car, and put it into his pocket. We walked over to the house, talking about various things, and they asked me where the windows of this man's apartment were. After I had showed them the place, one of them stayed outside and the other went in.

It did not take long. He came out with the father of the family. They led him over to the car and put handcuffs on him. When I saw that, I also knew what it was that the other man had grabbed before he left the car. It was a pistol and these men were from the Gestapo (secret police).

We later learned that the man was taken to a concentration camp in the area of Danzig. There they probably tried him, accusing him of having been a guerilla. Whether this was true or not, we don't know, but after two years of imprisonment, the family received the news that he had died of a lung infection. We also didn't know whether this was true or not, or whether he had been shot. Although he did not look healthy while he was working for us, it was perhaps more probable that he was executed than that he died a natural death.

The severest winter during the whole war was that of 1941-42. In fact, it was the severest that most of the old folks remembered. The troops may have been able to conquer Moscow, but the tanks and the soldiers were not prepared for such extreme temperatures, and the whole offense was shifted toward a defense position. When the winter started, the propaganda minister, Dr. Goebbels, sent around a proclamation that the German people should bring their extra phonograph records to a collection center that they might be packed and shipped to the front for the soldiers' entertainment.

Later, when the winter became more and more severe, the government made an appeal that everybody who had extra clothing, especially warm clothing, should donate it for the needy troops at the front lines; by then it was already almost too late. My father was quite upset that they first had collected records and then clothing. He felt, and I think most of the people agreed, that warm clothing was more necessary than records. In spite of that, most gave generously because they were experiencing at home what the winter meant.

ARMY RECRUITS

The longer the war continued, the heavier were the losses. Altogether Germany lost about six and a half million people, most of whom were soldiers. This required that many others be drafted into the army; whether they were fit or whether they were old enough did not play a big role. My oldest brother was drafted first and later on one of my other brothers received a draft order which he could not fulfill since he had injured his leg. The draft age went down to sixteen and a half years. As I was born in 1929, I would have probably been drafted at the end of 1945 if the war had lasted. The selective service and the various representatives of the armed forces were quite anxious to enlist us high school boys for the army officers' corps.

Most ambitious of all were the SS representatives. They were looking for tall, healthy, and intellectual, as well as politically well-developed, recruits. Although I was quite well indoctrinated with the Nazi ideas, I always felt a distaste for joining the SS troops. Occasionally representatives from various branches of the armed forces gave talks in our school and tried to enlist us into their respective branches. Navy officers wanted us to enlist as submarine or other naval officers. The army wanted officers, especially for the infantry, and promotion was the quickest in the infantry because of the heavy losses. In order to avoid all these over-ambitious recruiters, I signed up later with the artillery.

Almost monthly when we had an assembly period our high school principal read the roll of former students who had lost their lives for the country. Almost daily toward the end of the war there came reports from Hitler's headquarters that the army had to retreat here and there. One battleship after the other went down in the cold waters of the Atlantic. Although there was success here and there, there certainly was not much hope for one who saw clearly.

On the other hand, it was surprising how much trust and confidence (because of the constant propaganda) the people still had in their government, even though it was now fighting for a lost cause. Although West Germany was bombed day and night, and although Germany was flooded with foreign workers, and although there was a material shortage and a manpower shortage, everything seemed to be securely organized even to the last day. Nevertheless, the end was inevitable.

The revolt of the Badoglio Italians, the overthrow of Mussolini, the breakdown of the defense of Rumania, Bulgaria, Finland, Hungary, and Slovakia were certainly not things which pointed toward success. There was also resistance within Germany, men who sent water to the front lines instead of gasoline or who shipped wrong-fitting ammunition to the artillery. Supplies ran short, communications were destroyed by Allied bombing, and the bombing of living quarters in West and East Germany broke down the morale of the German people. There were people who were at that time opposed to Hitler's ideas of trying to fight to the last. An attempt to kill him on July 20, 1944, failed.

In one of the last speeches Hitler made, he mentioned at the close, "We will win the war, by the help of God!" Many religious people sat up saying: "Has our *Führer,* Adolf Hitler, turned to God again? Has God not forsaken us?" Others said, "We are a Christian nation. God will not allow atheistic Communism to overrun us. He will surely spare us somehow!"

But judgment was inevitable. There was no way out. Though the news was so highly propagandized that one could not tell real news from propaganda, even the casual observer should have been able to see the signs of the end on the horizon.